Language Art

Teacher's Guide

CONTENTS

Revision Editor: Alan Christopherson, M.S.

Alpha Omega Publications ®

300 North McKemy Avenue, Chandler, Arizona 85226-2618

CURRICULUM

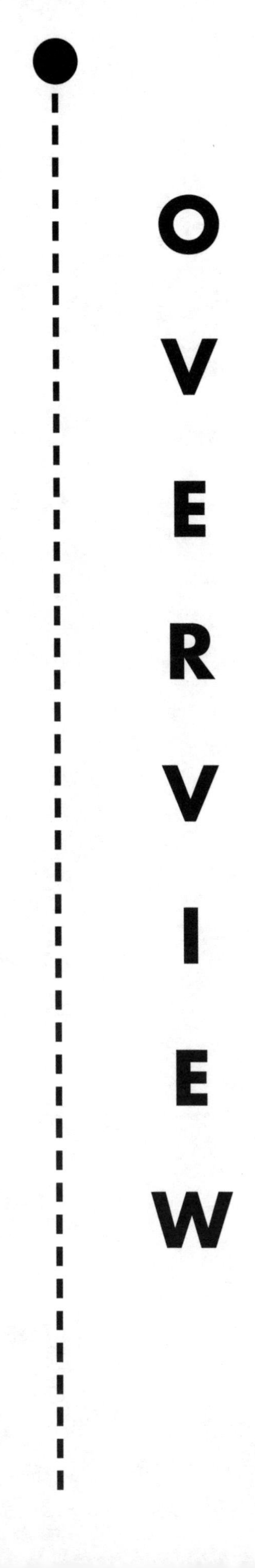

LANGUAGE ARTS

Curriculum Overview
Grades K–12

Kindergarten

Language Arts Lessons

1-40	41-80	81-120	121-160
Alphabet-say the alphabet **Colors**-recognize colors **Directions**-left to right **Following directions**-given once **Grammar**-form simple sentences **Listening skills** **Personal recognition**-read and write first name -know age and address -recognize names of family members **Phonics**-short *a, e, i* vowels -initial: *b, t, m, r, s, n, d, p, l* -form and read simple words -form rhyming words **Shapes**-circle, square, triangle, and rectangle -recognize shapes in objects **Stories and Poems**-create simple stories and poems **Writing**-form circle and lines -*Aa, Bb, Dd, Ee, Ii, Ll, Mm, Nn, Pp, Rr, Ss, and Tt*	**Grammar**-sentences begin with capital, end with period **Patterns**-simple shape, color patterns **Personal recognition**-read and write first and last name **Phonics**-short *a, e, i, o, and u* vowels -initial: *k, c, ck, f, h, g, j, v, w, y, z, qu, and x* -read simple sentences **Position/direction concepts**-in/out, in front of/behind, up/down, on/off, open/closed, over/under **Sequencing**-alphabetical order -simple story **Shapes**-oval **Size concepts**-big/little, large/small **Writing**-*Kk, Cc, Ff, Hh, Oo, Gg, Jj, Vv, Ww, Uu, Yy, Zz, Qq, and Xx*	**Phonics**-recognize the short vowel sounds -recognize all initial consonant sounds -recognize long *a, e, i, o,* and *u* sounds -silent *e* -initial consonant digraphs: *sh, ch,* both soft and hard *th* -final consonant sounds: *_b, _ck, _k, _l* **Word recognition**-color words, number words & shape words **Writing**-name -complete alphabet, capital and small letters -all color words -number words: *one, two, three, four, five, six* -shape words: *circle, square, triangle*	**Phonics**-recognize the long vowel sounds -initial consonant digraphs: *wh;* review *ch, sh, th* -recognize all final consonant sounds: **Stories and poems**-create, tell, and recite stories and poems **Word recognition**-position/direction words: *up/down, high/low, in, inside, out, outside, top/bottom* -number words: *seven, eight, nine, ten* -shape words: *rectangle, oval, star* **Writing**-number words: *seven, eight, nine, ten* -shape words: *rectangle, oval, star* -position/direction words: *up/down, high/low, in, inside, out, outside, top/bottom*

Language Arts LIFEPAC Overview

	Grade 1	Grade 2	Grade 3
LIFEPAC 1	FUN WITH PHONICS • Short vowel sounds • Consonants • Main ideas • Rhyming words	FROM SOUNDS TO WORDS • Talk • Write • Our alphabet • Vowels • Consonants	OLD AND NEW SKILLS • Vowels • Consonants • Sentence phrases • Capital letters • Reading skills
LIFEPAC 2	FUN WITH PHONICS • Kinds of sentences • Cardinal • Ordinal numbers • Suffixes • Plurals • Classifying	WORDS TO SENTENCES • Letters in words • Words in phrases • Words in sentences • Reading comprehension	BUILDING WORDS SENTENCES • Vowels - long, short • Questions • ABC order • Capital letters
LIFEPAC 3	FUN WITH PHONICS • Consonant digraphs • Compounds • Syllables • Possessives • Contractions • Soft c and g	HOW THE SENTENCE BEGINS • Sentences to talk • Sentences to write • Capital letters • Consonant blends	WORDS • GETTING TO THE ROOTS • Root words • Dictionary guide words • Synonyms • Antonyms • Capital letters
LIFEPAC 4	FUN WITH PHONICS • Paragraphs • Silent letters • Sequencing • Subject-verb agreement	A SECOND LOOK AT LETTERS • Capital letters • Consonant blends • Long vowels • Short vowels	WORDS • HOW TO USE THEM • Noun • Verb • Adjective •Adverb • Irregular vowels • Composition
LIFEPAC 5	FUN WITH PHONICS • Long vowels • Homonyms • Poetry • Syllables • Possessives • Contractions • Plurals • Suffixes	SENTENCE START TO FINISH • Ending punctuation • Capital letters • Digraphs • Creative writing	SENTENCE • START TO FINISH • Question marks • Commas • Periods • Paragraphs • Plural words
LIFEPAC 6	FUN WITH PHONICS • R-controlled vowels • Writing stories • Pronouns • Following directions	MORE ABOUT PUNCTUATION • Contractions • Digraphs • Vowel sounds • Dictionary • ABC order	ALL ABOUT BOOKS • Books • Stories • Poems • Card catalogue • Critical thinking
LIFEPAC 7	FUN WITH PHONICS • Vowel digraphs • Letters - business, friendly, invitations • Syllables	WORDS • GETTING TO THE ROOTS • Root words • Suffixes • Creative writing • More about the dictionary	READING AND WRITING • For directions • Friendly letters • Pronouns • Fact • Fiction
LIFEPAC 8	FUN WITH PHONICS • Vowel digraphs • Subject-verb agreement • Compounds • Contractions • Possessives •Pronouns	WORDS • BEGINNING & ENDING • Prefixes • Suffixes • Cursive handwriting • Creative writing • Dictionary	READING SKILLS • For sequence • For detail • Verbs - being, compound • Drama
LIFEPAC 9	FUN WITH PHONICS • Vowel digraphs • Titles • Main ideas • Sentences • Paragraphs • Proper nouns	WORDS • HOW TO USE THEM • Verbs - singular, plural • Verb tense • Creative writing • Dictionary	MORE READING & WRITING • For information • Thank you letters • Book reports • Reference books
LIFEPAC 10	LOOKING BACK • Letters and sounds • Contractions • Plurals • Possessives • Sentences • Stories	LOOKING BACK • Vowels • Consonants • Contractions • Compounds • Sentences • Phrases • Dictionary	LOOKING BACK • Reading for comprehension • Sentence punctuation • Writing letters • Parts of Speech

	Grade 4	Grade 5	Grade 6
LIFEPAC 1	WRITTEN COMMUNICATION • Word derivations • Story sequence • Writing an outline • Writing a report	STORY MESSAGES • Main idea • Plot • Character • Setting • Dialogue • Diphthong • Digraph	READING FOR A PURPOSE • Critical thinking • Research data • Parables • Synonyms
LIFEPAC 2	SOUNDS TO WORDS • Hard and soft – c and g • Parts of dictionary • Accented syllables • Haiku Poetry	MAIN IDEAS • Poetry • Story • Synonyms • Compounds • Topic sentence • Adjectives • Nouns	FORMING NEW WORDS • Prefixes • Suffixes • Synonyms • Antonyms • Adjectives • Adverbs • Critical thinking
LIFEPAC 3	WORDS • HOW TO USE THEM • Prefixes • Suffixes • Homonyms • Antonyms • Poetry • Stories • Writing an outline	WORDS TO STORIES • Subject • Predicate • Adverbs • Idioms • Critical thinking • Writing a short story	BETTER READING • Story elements • Author's purpose • Information sources • Outline
LIFEPAC 4	MORE WORDS • HOW TO USE THEM • Parts of speech • Possession • Written directions • Verb tenses	WRITTEN REPORT • Outline • Four types of sentences • Metaphor • Simile • Writing the report	SENTENCES • Capitals • Punctuation • Four types of sentences • Author's purpose • Propaganda
LIFEPAC 5	WRITING FOR CLARITY • Figures of speech • Capital letters • Punctuation marks • Writing stories	STORY ELEMENTS • Legend • Implied meaning • Dialogue • Quotations • Word order • Usage • Critical thinking	READING SKILLS • Following directions • Literary forms • Phrases • Nouns • Verbs • Paragraph structure
LIFEPAC 6	FUN WITH FICTION • Book reports • Fiction • Nonfiction • Parables • Fables • Poetry	POETRY • Rhythm • Stanza • Symbolism • Personification • Irregular plurals	POETRY • Similes • Metaphors • Alliteration • Homonyms • Palindromes • Acronyms • Figures of speech
LIFEPAC 7	FACT AND FICTION • Nouns • Verbs • Contractions • Biography • Fables • Tall Tales	WORD USAGE • Nouns - common, plural, possessive • Fact • Opinion • Story • Main idea	STORIES • Story elements • Nouns • Pronouns • Vowel digraphs • Business letter
LIFEPAC 8	GRAMMAR AND WRITING • Adjectives to compare • Adverbs • Figurative language • Paragraphs	ALL ABOUT VERBS • Tense • Action • Participles • Of being • Regular • Irregular • Singular • Plural	NEWSPAPERS • Propaganda • News stories • Verbs – auxiliary, tenses • Adverbs
LIFEPAC 9	THE WRITTEN REPORT • Planning a report • Finding information • Outline • Writing a report	READING FLUENCY • Speed reading • Graphic aids • Study skills • Literary forms	READING THE BIBLE • Parables • Proverbs • Hebrew - poetry, prophecy • Bible history • Old Testament law
LIFEPAC 10	LOOKING BACK • Reading skills • Nouns • Adverbs • Written communication • Literary forms	LOOKING BACK • Literary forms • Parts of speech • Writing skills • Study skills	LOOKING BACK • Literary forms • Writing letters • Parts of speech • Punctuation

Language Arts LIFEPAC Overview

	Grade 7	Grade 8	Grade 9
LIFEPAC 1	WORD USAGE • Nouns – proper, common • Pronouns • Prefixes • Suffixes • Synonyms • Antonyms	IMPROVE COMMUNICATION • Roots • Inflections • Affixes • Interjections • Directions – oral, written • Non-verbal communication	STRUCTURE OF LANGUAGE • Nouns • Adjectives • Verbs • Prepositions • Adverbs • Conjunctions • Sentence parts
LIFEPAC 2	MORE WORD USAGE • Speech – stress, pitch • Verbs – tenses • Principle parts • Story telling	ALL ABOUT ENGLISH • Origin of language • Classification– nouns, pronouns, verbs, adjectives, adverbs	NATURE OF LANGUAGE • Origin of language • Use – oral and written • Dictionary • Writing a paper
LIFEPAC 3	BIOGRAPHIES • Biography as a form • Flashback technique • Deductive reasoning • Words – base, root	PUNCTUATION AND WRITING • Connecting and interrupting • The Essay • Thesis Statement	PRACTICAL ENGLISH • Dictionary use • Mnemonics • Writing a paper • Five minute speech
LIFEPAC 4	LANGUAGE STRUCTURE • Verbs – tenses • Principle parts • Sentence creativity • Speech – pitch, accent	WORDS • HOW TO USE THEM • Dictionary • Thesaurus • Accent • Diacritical mark • Standard • Nonstandard	SHORT STORY FUNDAMENTALS • Plot • Setting • Characterization • Conflict • Symbolism
LIFEPAC 5	NATURE OF ENGLISH • Formal • Informal • Redundant expressions • Verb tenses • Subject–verb agreement	CORRECT LANGUAGE • Using good form • Synonyms • Antonyms • Homonyms • Good speaking qualities	LANGUAGE IN LITERATURE • Collective Nouns • Verbs • Use of comparisons • Gerunds • Participles • Literary genres
LIFEPAC 6	MECHANICS OF ENGLISH • Punctuation • Complements • Modifiers • Clauses – subordinate, coordinate	LANGUAGE AND LITERATURE • History of English • Coordination and Subordination • Autobiography	ENHANCED READING SKILLS • Author's message • Using Visual Aids – charts, graphs, tables • Understanding poetry
LIFEPAC 7	THE NOVEL • The Hiding Place • Sequence of events • Author's purpose • Character sketch	CRITICAL THINKING • Word evaluation • The Paragraph – structure, coherence, introductory, concluding	COMMUNICATION • Planning a speech • Listening comprehension • Letters – business, informal, social
LIFEPAC 8	LITERATURE • Nonfiction • Listening skills • Commas • Semicolons • Nonverbal communications	WRITE • LISTEN • READ • Business letters • Personal letters • Four steps to listen • Nonfiction	LIBRARY AND DRAMA • Library resources • Drama – history, elements, reading • The Miracle Worker
LIFEPAC 9	COMPOSITIONS • Sentence types • Quality of paragraph • Pronunciation • Nonsense literature	SPEAK AND WRITE • Etymology • Modifiers • Person • Number • Tense • Oral report	STUDIES IN THE NOVEL • History • Define • Write • Critical essay • Twenty Thousand Leagues Under the Sea
LIFEPAC 10	LOOKING BACK • Parts of speech • Sentence structure • Punctuation • How to communicate	LOOKING BACK • Composition structure • Parts of speech • Critical thinking • Literary forms	LOOKING BACK • Communication – writing speaking, listening • Using resources • Literature review

	Grade 10	Grade 11	Grade 12
LIFEPAC 1	EVOLUTION OF ENGLISH • Historical development • Varieties of English • Substandard & standard • Changes in English	ENGLISH USES • VARIETIES • Standard • Nonstandard • Professional • Literary • Lexicography – purpose, bibliography	THE WORTH OF WORDS • Word categories • Expository writing • Sentence structure • Diction
LIFEPAC 2	LISTENING AND SPEAKING • Noun plurals • Suffixes • Creating a speech • Nature of listening	EFFECTIVE SENTENCES • Subordinate – clauses, conjunctions • Relative pronouns • Verbals • Appositives	STRUCTURE OF LANGUAGE • Parts of speech • Sentence structure • Subordinate phrases • Subordinate clauses
LIFEPAC 3	EFFECTIVE SENTENCES • Participles • Infinitives • Prepositions • Gerunds • Sentences – simple, compound, complex	SENTENCE WORKSHOP • Pronouns – personal, reference, agreement • Misplaced modifiers • Parallel structure	READ, RESEARCH, LISTEN • Reading skills • Resources for research • Taking notes • Drawing conclusions
LIFEPAC 4	POWER OF WORDS • Etymology • Connotations • Poetic devices • Poetry – literal, figurative, symbolic	WHY STUDY READING? • Greek and Latin roots • Diacritical markings • Finding the main idea • Analyzing a textbook	GIFT OF LANGUAGE • Origin–Biblical, • Koine Greek • Purpose of Grammar • Semantics
LIFEPAC 5	ELEMENTS OF COMPOSITION • Paragraphs • Connectives • Transitions • Expository writing – elements, ideas	POETRY • Metrical feet • Sets • Musical effects • Universality • Imagery • Connotation	ENGLISH LITERATURE • Early England • Medieval England • Fourteenth century • Chaucer
LIFEPAC 6	STRUCTURE AND READING • Subordinate clauses • Pronouns – gender, case, agreement • Reading for recognition	NONFICTION • Elements • Types – essays, diaries, newspaper, biography • Composition	ELIZABETHAN LITERATURE • Poetry • Prose • Drama • Essay
LIFEPAC 7	ORAL READING AND DRAMA • Skills of oral reading • Drama – history, irony elements, allegory • Everyman	AMERICAN DRAMA • Development • History • Structure • Purpose • Our Town	17TH—18TH CENTURY LITERATURE • Historical background • Puritan literature • Common sense – satire • Sensibility
LIFEPAC 8	THE SHORT STORY • Elements • Enjoying • Writing • The Literary Critique	AMERICAN NOVEL • Eighteenth, nineteenth twentieth century • The Old Man and the Sea • The Critical Essay	WRITING • SHORT STORY, POETRY • Fundamentals • Inspiration • Technique and style • Form and process
LIFEPAC 9	THE NOVEL • Elements • In His Steps • The Critical Essay • The Book Review	COMPOSITION • Stating the thesis • Research • Outline • Writing the paper	POETRY • ROMANTIC , VICTORIAN • Wordsworth • Coleridge • Gordon • Byron • Shelley • Keats • Tennyson • Hopkins • Robert and Elizabeth B Browning
LIFEPAC 10	LOOKING BACK • Writing skills • Speech skills • Poetry • Drama • Short stories • Novel	LOOKING BACK • Analyzing written word • Effective sentences • Expository prose • Genres of American literature	LOOKING BACK • Creative writing • English literature – Medieval to Victorian

LIFEPAC

MANAGEMENT

STRUCTURE OF THE LIFEPAC CURRICULUM

The LIFEPAC curriculum is conveniently structured to provide one teacher handbook containing teacher support material with answer keys and ten student worktexts for each subject at grade levels two through twelve. The worktext format of the LIFEPACs allows the student to read the textual information and complete workbook activities all in the same booklet. The easy to follow LIFEPAC numbering system lists the grade as the first number(s) and the last two digits as the number of the series. For example, the Language Arts LIFEPAC at the 6th grade level, 5th book in the series would be LA 605.

Each LIFEPAC is divided into 3 to 5 sections and begins with an introduction or overview of the booklet as well as a series of specific learning objectives to give a purpose to the study of the LIFEPAC. The introduction and objectives are followed by a vocabulary section which may be found at the beginning of each section at the lower levels, at the beginning of the LIFEPAC in the middle grades, or in the glossary at the high school level. Vocabulary words are used to develop word recognition and should not be confused with the spelling words introduced later in the LIFEPAC. The student should learn all vocabulary words before working the LIFEPAC sections to improve comprehension, retention, and reading skills.

Each activity or written assignment has a number for easy identification, such as 1.1. The first number corresponds to the LIFEPAC section and the number to the right of the decimal is the number of the activity.

Teacher checkpoints, which are essential to maintain quality learning, are found at various locations throughout the LIFEPAC. The teacher should check 1) neatness of work and penmanship, 2) quality of understanding (tested with a short oral quiz), 3) thoroughness of answers (complete sentences and paragraphs, correct spelling, etc.), 4) completion of activities (no blank spaces), and 5) accuracy of answers as compared to the answer key (all answers correct).

The self test questions are also number coded for easy reference. For example, 2.015 means that this is the 15th question in the self test of Section II. The first number corresponds to the LIFEPAC section, the zero indicates that it is a self test question, and the number to the right of the zero the question number.

The LIFEPAC test is packaged at the centerfold of each LIFEPAC. It should be removed and put aside before giving the booklet to the student for study.

Answer and test keys have the same numbering system as the LIFEPACs and appear at the back of this handbook. The student may be given access to the answer keys (not the test keys) under teacher supervision so that he can score his own work.

A thorough study of the Curriculum Overview by the teacher before instruction begins is essential to the success of the student. The teacher should become familiar with expected skill mastery and understand how these grade level skills fit into the overall skill development of the curriculum. The teacher should also preview the objectives that appear at the beginning of each LIFEPAC for additional preparation and planning.

TEST SCORING and GRADING

Answer keys and test keys give examples of correct answers. They convey the idea, but the student may use many ways to express a correct answer. The teacher should check for the essence of the answer, not for the exact wording. Many questions are high level and require thinking and creativity on the part of the student. Each answer should be scored based on whether or not the main idea written by the student matches the model example. "Any Order" or "Either Order" in a key indicates that no particular order is necessary to be correct.

Most self tests and LIFEPAC tests at the lower elementary levels are scored at 1 point per answer; however, the upper levels may have a point system awarding 2 to 5 points for various answers or questions. Further, the total test points will vary; they may not always equal 100 points. They may be 78, 85, 100, 105, etc.

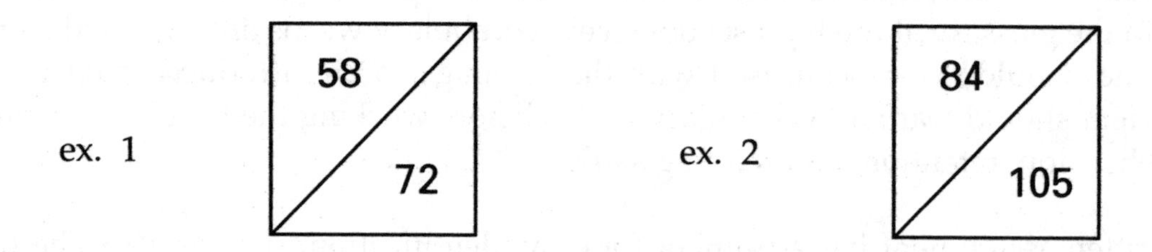

A score box similar to ex.1 above is located at the end of each self test and on the front of the LIFEPAC test. The bottom score, 72, represents the total number of points possible on the test. The upper score, 58, represents the number of points your student will need to receive an 80% or passing grade. If you wish to establish the exact percentage that your student has achieved, find the total points of his correct answers and divide it by the bottom number (in this case 72.) For example, if your student has a point total of 65, divide 65 by 72 for a grade of 90%. Referring to ex. 2, on a test with a total of 105 possible points, the student would have to receive a minimum of 84 correct points for an 80% or passing grade. If your student has received 93 points, simply divide the 93 by 105 for a percentage grade of 86%. Students who receive a score below 80% should review the LIFEPAC and retest using the appropriate Alternate Test found in the Teacher's Guide.

The following is a guideline to assign letter grades for completed LIFEPACs based on a maximum total score of 100 points.

LIFEPAC Test = 60% of the Total Score (or percent grade)
Self Test = 25% of the Total Score (average percent of self tests)
Reports = 10% or 10* points per LIFEPAC
Oral Work = 5% or 5* points per LIFEPAC
*Determined by the teacher's subjective evaluation of the student's daily work.

Example:

LIFEPAC Test Score	=	92%	92 x .60	=	55 points
Self Test Average	=	90%	90 x .25	=	23 points
Reports				=	8 points
Oral Work				=	4 points
TOTAL POINTS				=	90 points

Grade Scale based on point system:

100	–	94	=	A
93	–	86	=	B
85	–	77	=	C
76	–	70	=	D
Below		70	=	F

TEACHER HINTS and STUDYING TECHNIQUES

LIFEPAC Activities are written to check the level of understanding of the preceding text. The student may look back to the text as necessary to complete these activities; however, a student should never attempt to do the activities without reading (studying) the text first. Self tests and LIFEPAC tests are never open book tests.

Language arts activities (skill integration) often appear within other subject curriculum. The purpose is to give the student an opportunity to test his skill mastery outside of the context in which it was presented.

Writing complete answers (paragraphs) to some questions is an integral part of the LIFEPAC Curriculum in all subjects. This builds communication and organization skills, increases understanding and retention of ideas, and helps enforce good penmanship. Complete sentences should be encouraged for this type of activity. Obviously, single words or phrases do not meet the intent of the activity, since multiple lines are given for the response.

Review is essential to student success. Time invested in review where review is suggested will be time saved in correcting errors later. Self tests, unlike the section activities, are closed book. This procedure helps to identify weaknesses before they become too great to overcome. Certain objectives from self tests are cumulative and test previous sections; therefore, good preparation for a self test must include all material studied up to that testing point.

The following procedure checklist has been found to be successful in developing good study habits in the LIFEPAC curriculum.

1. Read the introduction and Table of Contents.
2. Read the objectives.
3. Recite and study the entire vocabulary (glossary) list.
4. Study each section as follows:
    a. Read the introduction and study the section objectives.
    b. Read all the text for the entire section, but answer none of the activities.
    c. Return to the beginning of the section and memorize each vocabulary word and definition.
    d. Reread the section, complete the activities, check the answers with the answer key, correct all errors, and have the teacher check.
    e. Read the self test but do not answer the questions.
    f. Go to the beginning of the first section and reread the text and answers to the activities up to the self test you have not yet done.
    g. Answer the questions to the self test without looking back.
    h. Have the self test checked by the teacher.
    i. Correct the self test and have the teacher check the corrections.
    j. Repeat steps a–i for each section.

5. Use the SQ3R* method to prepare for the LIFEPAC test.
6. Take the LIFEPAC test as a closed book test.
7. LIFEPAC tests are administered and scored under direct teacher supervision. Students who receive scores below 80% should review the LIFEPAC using the SQ3R* study method and take the Alternate Test located in the Teacher Handbook. The final test grade may be the grade on the Alternate Test or an average of the grades from the original LIFEPAC test and the Alternate Test.

   *SQ3R: Scan the whole LIFEPAC,
   Question yourself on the objectives,
   Read the whole LIFEPAC again,
   Recite through an oral examination, and
   Review weak areas.

GOAL SETTING and SCHEDULES

Each school must develop its own schedule, because no single set of procedures will fit every situation. The following is an example of a daily schedule that includes the five LIFEPAC subjects as well as time slotted for special activities.

Possible Daily Schedule

8:15	–	8:25	Pledges, prayer, songs, devotions, etc.
8:25	–	9:10	Bible
9:10	–	9:55	Language Arts
9:55	–	10:15	Recess (juice break)
10:15	–	11:00	Mathematics
11:00	–	11:45	Social Studies
11:45	–	12:30	Lunch, recess, quiet time
12:30	–	1:15	Science
1:15	–		Drill, remedial work, enrichment*

*Enrichment: Computer time, physical education, field trips, fun reading, games and puzzles, family business, hobbies, resource persons, guests, crafts, creative work, electives, music appreciation, projects.

Basically, two factors need to be considered when assigning work to a student in the LIFEPAC curriculum.

The first is time. An average of 45 minutes should be devoted to each subject, each day. Remember, this is only an average. Because of extenuating circumstances a student may spend only 15 minutes on a subject one day and the next day spend 90 minutes on the same subject.

The second factor is the number of pages to be worked in each subject. A single LIFEPAC is designed to take 3 to 4 weeks to complete. Allowing about 3-4 days for LIFEPAC introduction, review, and tests, the student has approximately 15 days to complete the LIFEPAC pages. Simply take the number of pages in the LIFEPAC, divide it by 15 and you will have the number of pages that must be completed on a daily basis to keep the student on schedule. For example, a LIFEPAC containing 45 pages will require 3 completed pages per day. Again, this is only an average. While working a 45 page LIFEPAC, the student may complete only 1 page the first day if the text has a lot of activities or reports, but go on to complete 5 pages the next day.

Long range planning requires some organization. Because the traditional school year originates in the early fall of one year and continues to late spring of the following year, a calendar should be devised that covers this period of time. Approximate beginning and completion dates can be noted on the calendar as well as special occasions such as holidays, vacations and birthdays. Since each LIFEPAC takes 3-4 weeks or eighteen days to complete, it should take about 180 school days to finish a set of ten LIFEPACs. Starting at the beginning school date, mark off eighteen school days on the calendar and that will become the targeted completion date for the first LIFEPAC. Continue marking the calendar until you have established dates for the remaining nine LIFEPACs making adjustments for previously noted holidays and vacations. If all five subjects are being used, the ten established target dates should be the same for the LIFEPACs in each subject.

FORMS

The sample weekly lesson plan and student grading sheet forms are included in this section as teacher support materials and may be duplicated at the convenience of the teacher.

The student grading sheet is provided for those who desire to follow the suggested guidelines for assignment of letter grades found on page 3 of this section. The student's self test scores should be posted as percentage grades. When the LIFEPAC is completed the teacher should average the self test grades, multiply the average by .25 and post the points in the box marked self test points. The LIFEPAC percentage grade should be multiplied by .60 and posted. Next, the teacher should award and post points for written reports and oral work. A report may be any type of written work assigned to the student whether it is a LIFEPAC or additional learning activity. Oral work includes the student's ability to respond orally to questions which may or may not be related to LIFEPAC activities or any type of oral report assigned by the teacher. The points may then be totaled and a final grade entered along with the date that the LIFEPAC was completed.

The Student Record Book which was specifically designed for use with the Alpha Omega curriculum provides space to record weekly progress for one student over a nine week period as well as a place to post self test and LIFEPAC scores. The Student Record Books are available through the current Alpha Omega catalog; however, unlike the enclosed forms these books are not for duplication and should be purchased in sets of four to cover a full academic year.

WEEKLY LESSON PLANNER

Week of:

Subject	Subject	Subject	Subject
Monday			
Subject	Subject	Subject	Subject
Tuesday			
Subject	Subject	Subject	Subject
Wednesday			
Subject	Subject	Subject	Subject
Thursday			
Subject	Subject	Subject	Subject
Friday			

WEEKLY LESSON PLANNER

Week of:

	Subject	Subject	Subject	Subject
Monday				
	Subject	Subject	Subject	Subject
Tuesday				
	Subject	Subject	Subject	Subject
Wednesday				
	Subject	Subject	Subject	Subject
Thursday				
	Subject	Subject	Subject	Subject
Friday				

Student Name ______________________ Year __________

Bible

LP #	Self Test Scores by Sections 1	2	3	4	5	Self Test Points	LIFEPAC Test	Oral Points	Report Points	Final Grade	Date
01											
02											
03											
04											
05											
06											
07											
08											
09											
10											

History & Geography

LP #	Self Test Scores by Sections 1	2	3	4	5	Self Test Points	LIFEPAC Test	Oral Points	Report Points	Final Grade	Date
01											
02											
03											
04											
05											
06											
07											
08											
09											
10											

Language Arts

LP #	Self Test Scores by Sections 1	2	3	4	5	Self Test Points	LIFEPAC Test	Oral Points	Report Points	Final Grade	Date
01											
02											
03											
04											
05											
06											
07											
08											
09											
10											

Student Name ______________________ Year ________

Mathematics

LP #	Self Test Scores by Sections 1	2	3	4	5	Self Test Points	LIFEPAC Test	Oral Points	Report Points	Final Grade	Date
01											
02											
03											
04											
05											
06											
07											
08											
09											
10											

Science

LP #	Self Test Scores by Sections 1	2	3	4	5	Self Test Points	LIFEPAC Test	Oral Points	Report Points	Final Grade	Date
01											
02											
03											
04											
05											
06											
07											
08											
09											
10											

Spelling/Electives

LP #	Self Test Scores by Sections 1	2	3	4	5	Self Test Points	LIFEPAC Test	Oral Points	Report Points	Final Grade	Date
01											
02											
03											
04											
05											
06											
07											
08											
09											
10											

TEACHER NOTES

INSTRUCTIONS FOR LANGUAGE ARTS

The LIFEPAC curriculum from grades two through twelve was written with the daily instructional material written directly in the LIFEPACs. The student is encouraged to read and follow his own instructional material thus developing independent study habits. The teacher should introduce the LIFEPAC to the student, set a required completion schedule, complete teacher checks, be available for questions regarding both subject content and procedures, administer and grade tests and develop additional learning activities as desired. Teachers working with several students may schedule their time so that students are assigned to a quiet work activity when it is necessary to spend instructional time with one particular student.

Language arts includes those subjects that develop the students' communication skills. The LIFEPAC approach to combining reading, spelling, penmanship, composition, grammar, speech and literature in a single unit allows the teacher to integrate the study of these various language arts subject areas. The variety and scope of the curriculum may make it difficult for students to complete the required material within the suggested daily scheduled time of forty-five minutes. Spelling, book reports and various forms of composition may need to be completed during the afternoon enrichment period.

Cursive handwriting is introduced in the second grade LIFEPAC 208 with regular practice following in succeeding LIFEPACs. Diacritical markings are defined in the third grade LIFEPAC 304. A pronunciation key including diacritical markings is provided after the vocabulary word lists in all subjects beginning with LIFEPAC 305.

This section of the language arts Teacher's Guide includes the following teacher aids: Index of Concepts, *Book Report Form*, *Books Read Chart*, Suggested and Required Material (supplies), and Additional Learning Activities.

The *Book Report Form* and the *Books Read Chart* may be duplicated for individual student use.

The Index of Concepts is a quick reference guide for the teacher who may be looking for a rule or explanation that applies to a particular concept. It does not identify each use of the concept in the various LIFEPACs. The concepts change by grade level with the emphasis on phonics and reading skills changing to spelling and grammar for the older students.

The materials section refers only to LIFEPAC materials and does not include materials which may be needed for the additional learning activities. Additional learning activities provide a change from the daily school routine, encourage the student's interest in learning and may be used as a reward for good study habits.

Concept	LIFEPAC	Section
Clauses	901	4,5
Comparisons - (adjective/adverb)	905	2
Composition		
report preparation	903	3
letter writing	907	3
critical essay	909	3
Diagramming Sentences	901	5
Dictionary Use	903	1
	908	1
Drama	908	2
"The Miracle Worker"	908	3
English - development of	902	2
Language - development of	902	1,2
Library Use	908	1
Listening Skills	907	2
Literary Forms (introduction to drama, novel, poetry, short story)	905	3
Mnemonics	902	3
	903	2
Novel - study of	909	1
20,000 Leagues	909	2
Parts of Speech		
adjectives	901	1
	905	2
adverbs	901	2
conjunctions	901	3
nouns	901	1
	905	1
prepositions	901	3
pronouns	901	3
verbs	901	2
	905	1
Phrases (gerund, infinitive, participial, appositive)	901	4
Plurals	901	1
Poetry	905	3
	906	3
Possessives	901	1
Prefixes	902	3
Pronunciation	903	1,2
Propaganda	906	1
Public Speaking	907	1
Reading Skills		
(generalizations, main idea, details, recognizing patterns, topic sentence)	904	1
(author's message, critical thinking, sequence)	906	1
Reference Works	908	1
Root Words	902	3
Sentence Structure (clauses/phrases, direct/indirect object, predicate adjective, predicate nominative, subject/predicate)	901	4,5
Story Fundamentals	904	2,3
	905	3

Concept	LIFEPAC	Section
Speech Preparation	907	1
Spelling Tips	902	3
	903	2
Suffixes	902	3
Visual Aids (statistics, graphs, charts)	906	2
Word Origins	903	2

Concept	LIFEPAC	Section

BOOK REPORT FORM

Title ______________________

Author ______________________

Illustrator ______________________

Number of Pages ______________________

Copyright Date ______________________

Fiction or Nonfiction ______________________

Your Name ______________________

Date ______________________

Principal Characters ______________________

____

____

Setting ______________________

Summary: A summary gives the important events of a story or book. It skips most of the details but a few make the report more interesting. The summary should be written in complete sentences.

____

Tell why you did or did not like the book.

____

Name: ____________________

BOOKS READ

Title: Author: Date:	Title: Author: Date:	Title: Author: Date:	Title: Author: Date:
Title: Author: Date:	Title: Author: Date:	Title: Author: Date:	Title: Author: Date:
Title: Author: Date:	Title: Author: Date:	Title: Author: Date:	Title: Author: Date:
Title: Author: Date:	Title: Author: Date:	Title: Author: Date:	Title: Author: Date:
Title: Author: Date:	Title: Author: Date:	Title: Author: Date:	Title: Author: Date:
Title: Author: Date:	Title: Author: Date:	Title: Author: Date:	Title: Author: Date:
Title: Author: Date:	Title: Author: Date:	Title: Author: Date:	Title: Author: Date:
Title: Author: Date:	Title: Author: Date:	Title: Author: Date:	Title: Author: Date:
Title: Author: Date:	Title: Author: Date:	Title: Author: Date:	Title: Author: Date:
Title: Author: Date:	Title: Author: Date:	Title: Author: Date:	Title: Author: Date:

Materials Needed for LIFEPAC

Required:

Suggested:
an available grammar text that provides sufficient coverage of interjections, the eighth part of speech

Additional Learning Activities

Section I Nouns and Adjectives

1. Point out the importance of grasping the fundamentals of communication—parts of speech, phrases, and sentences. These "tools" are the keys that unlock the secret of written communication. Emphasize also the value of increasing a student's vocabulary—both written and oral—because recent surveys prove that successful achievement is closely related to large and adequate vocabularies.
2. Divide the class into several groups. Assign each group a certain paragraph from a book, but first remove all the pronouns in the selection. Have each group fill in the blanks with the correct pronouns.
3. Let each student choose any one page from *Twenty Thousand Leagues under the Sea* (the novel they will read this year) or any other approved novel. Then have the students take the longest paragraph on the page they choose and label all the parts of speech in that paragraph.

Section II Verbs and Adverbs

1. Choose a paragraph from the novel chosen for the preceding activity and read it aloud to the class, leaving out all the verbs.
2. Divide the class into several groups and give each a copy of the same paragraph used in the preceding activity in which all of the verbs are left out. Have each group fill in the blanks with verbs of their own choosing. Then in class the groups go over papers and compare them with the original author's passage.
3. Assign each student a brief passage from *The Miracle Worker* or another approved play or book. Have them go through the scene, identify the verbs, and classify them according to tense, voice, mood, person, and number.

Section III Pronouns, Prepositions, and Conjunctions

1. Review the five kinds of pronouns—personal, relative, interrogative, demonstrative, and indefinite. Make certain that the students can distinguish between the five and identify them correctly in a sentence.
2. Divide the class into groups of three or four. Assign each a passage from a novel, short story, or newspaper article. Have the groups underline each pronoun, draw a line from the pronoun to its antecedent, and then circle the antecedent.
3. Let each student take two or three paragraphs from an encyclopedia, a history text, or any other textbook. Working with the passages of their choice, the students should underline every preposition, circle every object of a preposition and draw an arrow from each underlined preposition to its proper circled object.

Section IV Phrases and Clauses

1. Go over several papers from the independent project in Section III. In that exercise pronouns and objects were identified. These two, combined with any modifiers, make up a prepositional phrase. Point out some of these.
2. Divide the class into two groups. Have one group write a dozen or so sentences and read them aloud to the second group. The second group must then identify the appositive in each sentence and the noun to which it refers.
3. Let each student choose a paragraph from an approved novel, short story, magazine article, or textbook. The students should go through the paragraph, sentence by sentence and underline every main clause once and every dependent clause twice. Each student should draw an arrow from each subordinate clause to the word or phrase that it modifies (if applicable).

Section V Subjects, Predicates, and Complements

1. Pick five sentences from any source and diagram them on the blackboard. Go over each, identifying the function of each sentence. Try to vary the choice of sentences to include illustrations of predicate nominatives, predicate adjectives, direct objects, and indirect objects.
2. Divide the class into three groups. Have the first group compose five sentences to be diagramed. Let the second group diagram the sentences, and have the third group grade the diagraming and identify and explain errors, if any.

Materials Needed for LIFEPAC

Required:

Suggested:
The Holy Bible, King James Version
Dictionary; Bible dictionary

Additional Learning Activities

Section I What Is Language?

1. Bring to class a textbook for another language (French, Spanish, German, etc.). Share some of the vocabulary with the class, concentrating on words that are familiar to the students. Point out differences and similarities between English and this other language.
2. Divide the class into two groups. Using the activities from Section I as a basis, organize a game of literary charades. Let students from one side communicate nonverbally titles of certain novels, plays, or poems studied in class this year while the second group guesses the answers. Then reverse the roles and let the second group act out the titles while the first group guesses.
3. Have each student write a brief paper on one of the following topics:
   a. the importance of learning a second language,
   b. the differences in verbal and written communication, or
   c. the beginning of language or any other related subject.
4. Grade this paper according to the detailed guidelines given in Section III of "A Parent's Guide To Mastering LIFEPAC Management".

Section II How Did We Get Our Language?

1. Choose one of Chaucer's *Canterbury Tales* and read it to the class to illustrate the differences in Middle English and our language today.
2. Divide the class into several small groups. Give each group a paragraph or two from the Chaucer story. Let the students go through the passage and circle all the words whose spelling, meaning, or pronunciation have changed from Chaucer's time until now.

Section III How Shall We Use Language?

1. Take the King James Version of the Bible and read the chapter concerning the Tower of Babel (Genesis 11) aloud to the class. Then read the same episode from a modern version of the Bible. Discuss the obvious differences in the language used.
2. Have the students each make lists of ten or twelve slang words they currently use and bring those lists to class. Then let them trade lists and look up the words on the lists they receive in a standard dictionary. Discuss in class the differences between the literal and slang meanings of some of the more popular words.
3. Have each student choose a lengthy paragraph from an approved novel and go through that passage underlining all the words containing the six common English prefixes. The student should then list all the words he has underlined and look them up in a dictionary.

Materials Needed for LIFEPAC

Required:

Suggested:
Dictionary or thesaurus

Additional Learning Activities

Section I Pronunciation

1. Explain the use of a thesaurus stressing how proper use of such an aid can greatly increase a student's vocabulary and improve the quality of his written and oral communication. Make thesauruses available to the students; possibly pass around several copies during the explanation.
2. Divide the class into small groups of three to five students each. Make several lists of five words each taken from the vocabulary inventory in Section 1 of this LIFEPAC. Give one such list to each group and have them look up their five words in a thesaurus and list at least three substitute words for each of the five listed.
3. Have each student choose a few pages from a novel, short story, or a drama that the class has read this year. The students should then go through their selection and underline all the unfamiliar words they find. After listing the underlined words, each student should then look them up in a dictionary and record their meanings and proper pronunciation.

Section II Spelling

1. Hold a class spelling bee using the words in the vocabulary inventory in Section I.
2. Divide the students into groups of two each. Give each group a different brief passage from any source you choose. Have the first student dictate the passage to the second, and then let the first student grade the second's dictation for spelling and punctuation. Then trade passages among the groups, have the students exchange roles, and repeat the exercise.
3. Have each student make a list of the twenty words he most often misspells. Then, using the techniques taught in the first two sections of this LIFEPAC, let each student devise a rule for correctly spelling each of his problem words. (If time permits, these lists could be exchanged and shared with the entire class.)

Section III Writing

1. Review in class the steps for preparing to write a paper, including choosing a topic, doing the research, outlining, and so forth. Encourage the students to ask questions about any part of the prewriting process that they do not readily understand at this point.
2. Assign a single topic and have each student write a brief outline for a five hundred-word paper on that topic. Let the students exchange outlines with their neighbors and grade each other's work. Point out that they should look for parallel construction, correct spelling and punctuation, and a logical ordering of the material to be covered.
3. Have each student listen to a speech outside of class (on television, in another class, at a local church or service organization meeting) and take notes during the speech. Students should then prepare a brief oral report criticizing the speech they heard. Such criticism should include the following points:
   a. Did the speaker cover the subject he said he would?
   b. Did he use correct English and proper pronunciation?
   c. Did he use transitions between points?
   d. Was his style of speaking effective?
   e. Did he accomplish his purpose?

Materials Needed for LIFEPAC

Required:

Suggested:
any book or magazine (another textbook will do)
The Holy Bible, King James Version

Additional Learning Activities

Section I Basic Reading Skills

1. Discuss the use of slang, colloquial language, obsolete words, substandard speech, dialect, and Biblical and standard English. Be sure to point out when each type is properly used in writing and speaking. Certain kinds of dialect, for example, lend reality to works of fiction but have no place at all in a formal nonfiction essay.
2. Go through one of the LIFEPAC stories having the students pick out the main idea in each paragraph. The class could be divided into several groups with each group assigned a certain number of paragraphs, or the exercise could be done with the class as a whole participating orally.
3. Six patterns are used for organizing supporting details in a paragraph. Have each student choose any two of these patterns and write two paragraphs, one which uses the first pattern he chose and one which uses the second. As always, spelling, punctuation, sentence structure, and capitalization are important in grading; but equally important in this assignment is the student's ability to properly develop his paragraph by the chosen method. Such development will prove that he has mastered the various kinds of organizing patterns for paragraphs in composition.

Section II Short Story Fundamentals

1. Using the story, "Flowers for Algernon" (or any other you choose), go through the text step by step in class and identify the six elements of a short story present in this particular work. Example: The characters are Charlie Gordon, Algernon the rat, . . . The plot is . . . and so forth.
2. Divide the class into groups of four or five. Have each group develop a list of possible symbols to use in a short story. (Note: six or eight symbols should be sufficient for each list.) Then let each group share their list with the rest of the class, explaining, when necessary, the underlying meanings of the symbols they have created. This exercise will encourage individual thinking and help to explain just how the literary process of symbolism works.
3. Have each student choose any Biblical story (other than those given in the LIFEPAC) and go through it to identify the six basic elements just as the class did in the first activity of this section. A written list of these elements should be turned in for grading.

Section III Two Short Stories

1. Choose any other short story and read it aloud to the class.
2. Now divide the class into five groups and assign each group a certain topic to discuss concerning the story you have just read them. Topics for discussion include these possibilities.
    a. Identify and explain the plot of the story.
    b. Locate the figurative language in the story and explain its effect.
    c. Explain the contribution of the setting to the story.
    d. Identify the characters and classify them according to type—round, flat, static, or dynamic.
    e. Explain the author's theme and the method he chose to state it (direct? implied?).

    After each group has finished its discussion, let members choose one representative to present group conclusions orally to the rest of the class.
3. Have each student choose a short story not discussed in class and read it as an outside assignment. Then let him pick any one of the following topics and write a brief (2-page) paper on the subject he chooses:
    a. the symbolism in the story,
    b the theme of the story,
    c. the author's use of figurative language in his work,
    d. the method the author chooses to draw his characters, or
    e. the importance of the setting or atmosphere to the story.

Materials Needed for LIFEPAC

Required:

Suggested:
Dictionary
The Holy Bible, King James Version

Additional Learning Activities

Section I Language in Daily Use

1. Select a newspaper and pass out copies to each student. Then using a preselected article, have student circle all collective nouns. If any are used with incorrect verbs or pronouns, have students make such note so that the class may take it as an example. Do the same for irregular verbs.
2. Give students a mimeographed copy of ten sentences, each containing double negatives or double comparisons. Have students work in pairs for ten minutes as they correct the errors, then have the students put the corrected versions on the blackboard.
3. Students may wish to read a selected short story and present a brief oral report to the class. Besides the usual critique of plot, characters, and theme, you may wish to have students comment upon the language. If so, prepare a few questions for the students to answer, otherwise, students will not be likely to complete the assignment to your satisfaction.

Section II Understanding Comparisons

1. Using an anthology, direct students to turn to a teacher-selected essay or short story. Have students look for comparisons. An alternate activity would be to use Proverbs from the Bible
2. Using either an anthology or the Bible, have students work in pairs and turn to a teacher-selected chapter or poem. Using Lindsay's poem, "The Broncho" as a guide, have students underline participles and gerunds, noting whether each example is a participle or a gerund. If you prefer, students may use a separate sheet of paper.
3. Have students write a brief poem using participles, nouns, and adjectives. This poetic form is called "diamante" because of its diamond shape. The particular arrangement of words, the mood change, and the number of words per line must be the same as this example.

Noun	MAFATU
Adjectives	AFRAID ALONE
Participles	CRYING MENDING ENVYING
Nouns	SHAME ANGER TERROR LONELINESS
Adjectives	WALKING HEARING PLANNING
Participles	BRAVE HONORABLE
Noun	HERO

The first and last nouns represent the same person or thing. The poem represents a change from first to last. The first group of adjectives and participles describe a certain mood which reaches its peak in line four. Line five consists of participles reflecting a change in mood. Line six contains different adjectives, describing a changed person or thing named in line seven.

Section III Literary Genres

1. The LIFEPAC suggests only one type of figure of speech—onomatopoeia, using a word whose sound suggests its meaning. Discuss other figures of speech with your class: metaphors (direct comparisons) and similes (direct comparisons), personification, alliteration.
2. With students working in two's or three's, have them devise figures of speech. The exercise works best with rather close teacher supervision. Suggest, for example, that students compose similes (sometimes humorous or outlandish ones produce the most indelible results for students' comprehension). Give them four or five minutes to write several, then call on several students to share their favorite example. Continue in a similar manner throughout the other figures of speech. A light touch often makes this kind of exercise more palatable for students (and teachers).
3. Suggest that students read a variety of short stories. As they find a favorite author (students often like Edgar Allen Poe, Katherine Mansfield, Ray Bradbury, O. Henry, Saki, Ernest Hemingway, F. Scott Fitzgerald, and De Maupassant), encourage them to read widely from that author's collected works.
4. Students may want to attempt to write a short story in the style of the author they have grown to enjoy. This exercise is valuable in teaching the concept of style and is an indirect method of leading into such a consideration or discussion.
5. Another possibility would be an oral report, sharing characteristics of the author's style and brief plots of two or three stories.

Materials Needed for LIFEPAC

Required:	Suggested:
World Book Dictionary	
poetry anthology	
The Holy Bible, King James Version	

Additional Learning Activities

Section I. Determining the Author's Message

1. If someone is in your locality associated with the NCTE (National Council of Teachers of English) Committee on Doublespeak, invite them to address your class. You may outline specific areas you wish covered.
2. Students may work in small groups to compose examples of propaganda techniques. Each group could be assigned a separate technique to illustrate to the class.
3. You may ask students to bring in an example of each of six propaganda techniques. Students should use magazines and newspapers but could also cite examples from daily living.
4. Students may create their own advertisement for "Krunchy Flakes Cereal" or "Sudz Duz" detergents.

Section II. Using Visual Aids

1. You may hand out sheets to the students. These sheets should contain logical, well organized paragraphs into which you have inserted one to three irrelevant ideas or sentences. Ask the students to read the paragraphs silently, then have a volunteer read the paragraph. Other students may then volunteer to locate the inconsistencies and irrelevancies.
2. You may scramble a formerly well organized paragraph—either the sentences may be cut apart or the material may be retyped in a poorly organized illogical manner. Students may work in pairs to correct the material. This activity would be a good time to review the concepts of topic sentences, transitions, and conclusions.
3. Students may design one of the four history, social studies, science, or grammar LIFEPACS.

Section III. Understanding Poetry

1. Ask students to bring a poem which they have enjoyed or which has special meaning to them. Stress the voluntary aspect of this assignment. Peer enjoyment will do far more than the threat of a grade to help students appreciate poetry. Ask students who are willing to read their selections aloud. Stress a natural reading manner; poetry is conversational.
2. Divide into six or eight small groups. Assign each group the same meter and rhyme scheme. Let the class decide on a topic or subjects that can be described chronologically or spatially. Then give the students ten or fifteen minutes to compose two lines of verse matching the set scheme. Each group should work on a particular aspect of the whole subject. Finally have the students put the lines in order, on the board. You may wish to type this poem as a class handout.
3. You may find it worth while to ask students to start a poetry journal; they can record the poems they find especially meaningful. This activity could be an extended project wherein students write original (or find published) poetry on a particular topic: charity, love, peace, and so forth. Make certain students give bibliographical references to the poets.

Materials Needed for LIFEPAC

Required: *World Book Dictionary*

Suggested:

Additional Learning Activities

Section I. Speaking

1. Students may be encouraged to enter speech forensics. If your school has no speech club, the teacher may wish to initiate one, perhaps seeking local or regional affiliation.
2. If your area has a Toastmaster's Club, students may (with the teacher's permission and advance arrangement with the club) wish to visit a meeting. Another possibility would be to invite members to the classroom so they could share speech pointers with the students.
3. If you know of a student who has won a local or regional speech contest, invite that student into the classroom to share ideas and speech-related experiences. Some of the students may wish to interview the guest speaker as an independent activity.
4. Encourage students to speak in extemporaneous speeches (write nonsense words or funny combinations like "blue-speckled honey-creepers" or current event phrases on cards; students can draw cards at the moment they are called on; they have just a few seconds to compose thoughts and then begin speaking, perhaps about the history, care, and future of "blue-speckled honey creepers." This kind of activity initially creates stress, so be compassionate. The result, though, leads to a quickening of wits and an ability to think immediately through a situation. Biblical passages as well as classroom concepts could, of course, be substituted.

Section II. Listening

1. Since speaking and listening are companion skills, the improvement of one leads to the improvement of the second. Students may desire to improve the quality of their voices, making it more pleasant for others to listen. If tape recorders are available, students may record themselves as they tell a story; the teacher may give suggestions about breathing more deeply and consciously trying to lower the voice. If there is a music teacher available, he may give further suggestions.
2. Students may take turns telling a favorite childhood or Bible story. They should prepare the storytelling outside of class, thinking about order, emphasis, and details. Material from the LIFEPAC regarding voice quality may be reread. If students wish, they may record themselves on cassettes to learn how to improve their voices. The storytelling itself, however, should be presented live to encourage interaction among the students.
3. Some students may like to visit an elementary classroom and complete the preceding activity for a younger audience.

Section III Letter Writing

1. Students may be asked to attend a lecture or a sermon where they may take notes after reviewing Section II.
2. Students may be asked to bring one or two business letters to class. Preferably these should be letters the family or student have received (nothing personal, please) and the salutation and address may be cut off or blacked out, if desired for privacy. The letters may be classified according to purpose, then discussed in light of the "A,B,C's" of business letter writing (accuracy, brevity, and clarity). If you wish, some of the examples may be copied so that they may be distributed for individual reading.
3. Students may wish to compose an informal social note, written as a group. Perhaps a note of congratulations, condolences, or appreciation might be in order.
4. If guests have been invited into the classroom, students may write social thank-you notes to those people.

Materials Needed for LIFEPAC

Required:	Suggested:
access to a library with a card catalog, encyclopedias, atlases, bibliographies, biographies, *Readers' Guide*, and dictionaries	

Gibson, William. *The Miracle Worker*. New York: Bantam Books, Inc., no date (or any available edition).

Additional Learning Activities

Section I. The Library

1. Ask students to choose one of the following topics:
   a. William Shakespeare;
   b. classical drama;
   c. mystery, morality, or miracle play;
   d. Anne Sullivan Macy;
   e. stage (set or scene) design;
   f. a career in library work (such as general library, research, special collections, administration), in special education (such as physical therapy, speech therapy, rehabilitation, mental retardation, administration, teaching, research, social work), or in theater (such as acting, playwriting, directing, technical design—costume, set lighting–law, management, teaching, children's theater). Then have each student go to the subject cards and find one book on the topic, copying down on a 3" x 5" index card the information as follows:

call number of book	Last name of author, first name
	title of book (underlined)
	place of publishing
	publisher
	date of publishing
	page numbers, if applicable

   This activity will lead directly to research papers if desired.
2. To illustrate graphically the cross-indexing of books, next have students find the same book in the author cards and also in the title cards. It would also be helpful to have the students locate the books on the shelves, since it shows how to use the catalog.
3. You might also consider inviting professionals from the career fields mentioned to speak to your students providing them with some additional awareness of career possibilities.
4. Small groups of students with similar career interests could invite a guest speaker into the classroom to share information and answer questions. Be sure to have students write thank-you notes (studied in LIFEPAC, 907).
5. Use the suggested topics from Section I for oral or written presentations.

Section II. Drama

1. Have the students locate one of the articles listed by Gibson in the *Readers' Guide.* After reading the critique each student may write a brief precis, summarizing the main points of the article, or he may give a brief oral report. This would be a good opportunity to stress a thesis statement and supplementary development of a theme. If expository writing has included patterns of theme development, this type would also be a possibility for a comparison-contrast theme.
2. If the size of your town or city permits, have students attend a teacher-selected play. They may then write reviews in small groups or individually. Additionally, you may collect a series of newspaper reviews about plays, lectures, or movies (some church publications also carry critiques of secular and religious films). News magazines offer well written reviews, too. These reviews may be copied so students will have samples to consult before writing their own critiques.
3. If you wish, you may invite a local critic into the classroom to give the students some pointers on critiquing a play. Sometimes, too, actors from a college or professional play will attend the class, offering insights valuable to the students and serving as stimuli for further enjoying and understanding the play.
4. It may be possible for one or two of the students to have their critiques selected for publication in a local newspaper.
5. A student may wish to give a brief "definition" paper, writing only one or two paragraphs based on the origin and development of either *tragedy* or *thespian.* (*Tragedy* evolves from classical Greek, meaning *goat-song*. *Thespian* refers to Thespis, the traditional father of Greek tragedy (sixth century B.C.) and therefore refers to tragedy or the dramatic arts.)

Section III. *The Miracle Worker*

1. Refer students to the quote opening Section III of the LIFEPAC. Ask whether they agree with the initial statement by Shaw that there is no such thing as a great man or woman. (For purposes of discussion omit discussion of Christ, the prophets, and Biblical heroes.) Do students find the concluding sentence inspirational? Have students known outstanding people? What are the characteristics of those people? How can students learn from them?
2. Students may be able to view a production of The *Miracle Worker*. If a live production is not available, you may be able to schedule a showing of the film. Following the guidelines for the Activity of Section II (writing a critique), students may work in pairs, writing a review of the play or the film.
3. Students may wish to turn *The Miracle Worker* into a short story (caution them about using too much exposition; keep the story lively) or into a poem-either a narration of the events or perhaps a reaction to the "miracle" of speech.

Materials Needed for LIFEPAC

Required:
Verne, Jules. *Twenty Thousand Leagues under the Sea*. New York: Bantam Books, Inc., no date (or any available edition).

Suggested:
The Holy Bible, King James Version

Additional Learning Activities

Section I The Novel

1. Bring to class a copy of one of the first novels—*Pamela, Joseph Andrews, Tristram Shandy* or one written at a slightly later time and read a few brief passages aloud to the students. Point out some of the differences between this work and a modern novel. (Examples: the kind of language, the form of the book, the author directly addressing the reader, etc.)
2. Locate and bring to class seven novels, each one representing one of the seven types of books—gothic, historic, detective, and so forth. Divide the class into seven groups and give each group one book to examine and discuss. Then have each group choose a spokesman and report to the class. (Possible points to include are the plot of the work, the setting, the theme, the kind of characters in the story, the point of view, and the symbolism if any.)
3. Let each student choose one of the five modes of writing a novel and then locate (through the card catalogue at the library) four novels that fit into that mode. If time permits, have the students share their lists with each other.
   Example: realism
   a. William Dean Howells' *Silas Lapham*
   b. Henry James' *The Bostonians*
   c. Stephen Crane's *The Red Badge of Courage*
   d. Frank Norris' *The Octopus*

Section II *Twenty Thousand Leagues under the Sea*

1. The value of any novel can only be evaluated if its theme is understood. Lead a class discussion concerning the theme (if any) of this Jules Verne novel. Is it directly stated in the work, and if so, where and how?
2. Pick a scene from the novel used in the preceding activity and stage it in class, assigning students the roles of various characters in the novel. If possible, pick a scene with three or more characters involved.
3. Have each student choose a second novel and read it outside of class. Then have the students do one of the following exercises with the book of their choice:
   a. Pick any three characters in the book, classify them as static or dynamic and then explain the various methods the author chose to develop those characters.
   b. Outline the basic plot of the story arranging all the important incidents in the order of occurrence. Be sure to include the crisis, or climax, and resolution.
   c. Symbolism is an important literary tool. Identify the important symbols in your novel and explain their purpose in the book.

Section III The Critical Essay

1. Choose any piece of literary criticism and read it aloud to the class. The choice could be an accepted, well known essay (example: Henry James's "The Art of Fiction") or a brief piece of modern criticism (often found in the book review section of magazines or newspaper Sunday supplements).
2. Set up a panel discussion about the criticism that was read aloud in the preceding activity. Some points to consider include these: Does any of this criticism apply to *Twenty Thousand Leagues under the Sea*? How was the essay organized? What was the thesis and how was it supported or proved (or was it)?
3. Have each student choose a critical essay and read it outside of class. A written report is unnecessary, but each student should take notes and organize them in order to be able to present a brief oral report covering the main points of the essay he or she read.

Materials Needed for LIFEPAC

Required:
Students should have access to all the English 900 LIFEPAC series for further information and review.
World Book Dictionary
a thesaurus

Suggested:

Additional Learning Activities

Section I Structure

1. Since dialects of English form a contemporary parallel to the background and history of English, the teacher may ask students to interview family and friends for examples of dialectical variations within the United States. Examples include *pot, skillet, pan, spider,* and *frypan.* Ask students what (if anything) they call the strip of lawn in front of a house, outside the front lawn or yard, and between the sidewalks and the curb. This introduction provides an interesting means of launching the discussion. Some students may call it a "boulevard"; others may not have a term for it.
2. Have students consult a text on *History of the English Language.* Let the students skim the text finding a section of language history that interests them. They may prepare a one- or two-page summary of the chapter to share with the class.

Section II Communication

1. The class may be divided into four or five groups. (Have students "count off" to eliminate "choosing" students.) Have a student from each group go to the blackboard and write a sentence that you dictate to them. Then, at your direction, have students diagram the sentence. First one to diagram the sentence correctly stands the next group representative.
2. Have students work in small groups. Each group will present a process speech—how to make a cake, change a tire, build a sidewalk. Students should cooperate to decide upon a topic, outline the presentation, then present the process, chronologically, to the class. Each group member should take part in the presentation. Visual aids may be used if you wish.
3. Have students write either to a state or federal agency requesting specific material to be used in the student's research paper. Some students may wish to write the Library of Congress for information.
4. Have students write a letter to the editor of your local newspaper or newspapers. Give extra credit if the letter is published.

Section III Reading

1. Often a little time is left in class—so little that you hesitate to start a new activity, yet hate to waste the time. Other times, an assembly or meeting may cut into class time and otherwise leave your students ill-prepared to study or to work. It is a good idea to read to the students, choosing perhaps an American or British classic like *The Scarlet Letter, The Last of the Mohicans,* or *Great Expectations*. Many students have never been read to, and consequently they have missed a great deal of joy and entertainment and beauty. While you may find students a little restless occasionally, you will probably find they will clamor for you to resume reading—assuming, of course, the book is interesting. (Perhaps the students could suggest or vote on selections.) If you choose to read, this activity will present an opportunity for you to be a role-model of a good speaker (and listener, at times). You may wish to read over the suggestions in LIFEPAC 907, to improve your own voice and reading techniques.
2. Many teachers find that students "catch" the habit of reading. It is a habit that can be encouraged by providing opportunities, in class, for students to read. Many teachers set every Friday aside as a "Reading Day." Students know they are expected to bring a book to class and they will read all period. It is important that students not be excused to go to the library; that can quickly undermine your plans. Also, it is absolutely necessary that you also read. Do not grade papers, catch up on classroom chores, or do anything else but *read*. It is necessary that students have a role-model because many come from nonreading homes. While this time may seem unstructured and wasteful, it is perhaps some of the most important time students spend in the classroom. Studies repeatedly and consistently show that students who read do better in school and score higher on college entrance exams.
3. Students may work in small groups to devise various games using literary terms. These games may be based upon Monopoly or Scrabble, but it is best to let the students' imaginations have free reign; do not constrict the students with *your* ideas of what the game should be like. They may surprise you with their ingenuity.
4. You may ask (or students may volunteer) that students provide a tour of the library to incoming freshmen. Since this review comes at the last part of the year, it may be convenient to provide an eighth-grade orientation. If so, your students--and the librarian--may provide a real service to the students and the school.

Notes

ALTERNATE

TESTS & KEYS

Reproducible Tests
for use with the Language Arts
900 Teacher's Guide

Name ________________________

Answer *true* or *false* (each answer, 1 point).

1. _______ Nouns are naming words.
2. _______ All common nouns begin with a capital letter.
3. _______ A compound subject is one that contains two or more simple subjects.
4. _______ A predicate adjective is a word that renames the subject.
5. _______ An adverb modifies a verb, an adjective, or another adverb.
6. _______ A prepositional phrase consists of a preposition, its object, and all modifiers of that object.
7. _______ The plural of most nouns is formed by adding *es*.
8. _______ Pronouns are words used in the place of nouns.
9. _______ Three kinds of verb forms function as phrases in sentences.
10. _______ Another name for a dependent clause is *subordinate clause*.

Match these items (each answer, 2 points).

11. _______ abstract noun
12. _______ tense
13. _______ conjugation
14. _______ participle
15. _______ compound sentence
16. _______ antecedent
17. _______ gerund
18. _______ adjective clause
19. _______ predicate
20. _______ conjunction
21. _______ possessive case
22. _______ transitive verb

a. arrangement of verb forms by tense, voice, mood, person, and number
b. contains two or more main clauses
c. the verb of a clause
d. a verb's time of action
e. shows ownership
f. shows action with an object
g. intransitive verb
h. a verb that functions as an adjective
i. specific noun to which a pronoun refers
j. a verb functioning as a noun
k. subordinate clause
l. connecting word
m. names something you cannot see or touch

Complete these statements (each answer, 3 points).

23. The most common mood used in English is the ______________ mood.
24. The two kinds of prepositional phrases found in sentences are
    a. ____________________ and b. ____________________ phrases.
25. A verbal phrase that can be used as a noun, adverb, or adjective and is preceded by the word *to* is a/an ____________________.
26. A noun or pronoun that follows another noun or pronoun to identify or explain the first one is a/an ____________________.
27. A sentence with one main clause and one or more dependent clauses is a ____________________ sentence.
28. A subordinate clause functions in a sentence as a ____________________.
29. The simple predicate of a sentence plus all its modifiers is called the ____________________.
30. The word or words that receive the action of a verb in a sentence is the ____________________.
31. A word used in a sentence to complete the meaning of the verb is a/an ____________________.
32. A noun that names a group of more than one person or things is a ____________________ noun.

Write the letter for the correct answer on each line (each answer, 2 points).

33. Love and happiness are both examples of ______________ nouns.
    a. concrete
    b. abstract
    c. proper
    d. common
34. The highest or lowest degree of comparison between three or more nouns is the ______________ degree.
    a. superlative
    b. real
    c. positive
    d. possessive

35. *Active* and *passive* are the two ______________ of verbs in a sentence.
   a. moods
   b. tenses
   c. voices
   d. groups
36. Pronouns that refer to inanimate objects are in the ______________ gender.
   a. neuter
   b. neither c nor d
   c. feminine
   d. masculine
37. A verbal phrase that functions in a sentence as an adjective is a ______________ phrase.
   a. gerund
   b. pronoun
   c. infinitive
   d. participle
38. A sentence with two or more main clauses and one or more subordinate clauses is a ______________.
   a. simple
   b. complex
   c. compound-complex
   d. compound

Diagram the following sentences (each answer, 5 points).

39. The boy hit the baseball into left field.

40. The girl with the purple dress took her mother to the concert.

71/89

Date ______________
Score ______________

Language Arts 902 Alternate Test

Name ____________________

Match these items (each answer, 2 points).

1. _______ origin of language
2. _______ syntax
3. _______ Babel
4. _______ phonology
5. _______ tongues
6. _______ nonverbal

a. dealing with sounds in words
b. language without words
c. another word for language
d. archaeology
e. confused languages
f. as early as man
g. having to do with word order

Answer *true* or *false* (each answer, 1 point).

7. _______ When Adam was first created, God communicated with him.
8. _______ All languages have the same thought patterns.
9. _______ From the time of Creation until the Tower of Babel, everyone spoke one language.
10. _______ English is considered a melting pot of several languages.
11. _______ Indo-European languages have clearly defined parts of speech.

Write the correct letter and answer on each line (each answer, 2 points).

12. Anthropology is the science that studies ________________.
    a. cities c. animals
    b. man d. geography
13. Archaeology is the science that studies ______________.
    a. cities c. the stars
    b. animals d. man
14. The root word *graph* means to ______________.
    a. speak c. write
    b. draw d. read
15. The following prefix means *not* : ______________.
    a. *em -* c. *ill -*
    b. *it -* d. *ir -*
16. The term *Aryans* actually refers to ______________.
    a. an ancient city c. a historic place
    b. an ancient language d. prehistoric people
17. A great tower has been uncovered at Ur, an ancient city of ___________.
    a. Iran c. Mesopotamia
    b. Afghanistan d. Wycliffe
18. Today almost all Europeans speak ______________ tongue.
    a. an Indu c. an Iranian
    b. an Aryan d. a Celtic

19. Words of Latin origin make up ______ percent of the English language.
    a. 50 c. 35
    b. 65 d. 25
20. English has about __________ million speakers.
    a. 225 c. 100
    b. 350 d. 90
21. All of the following languages are Celtic *except* ____________.
    a. Welsh c. Greek
    b. Briton d. Gaelic
22. The Genesis account of Creation assumes ____________ to be the source of language.
    a. Adam c. God
    b. man d. science

Complete these statements (each answer, 3 points).

23. We use the King James Version of the Bible because it is beautifully written and because it is true to the original a. ____________ and b. ____________ translations.
24. The word *peculiar* was used in 1611 to mean a very ____________ person or thing.
25. Noah's involved language structure is obvious because of the detailed and complicated ____________ he received about the ark.
26. A great variety of languages developed following the confusion of tongues at ____________.
27. By studying ____________, a student can improve his understanding and spelling of the English language.
28. The languages spoken at Babel were probably only ____________ languages.
29. The Normans merged French with ________________.

Answer this question (this answer, 5 points).

30. What is meant by the Great Vowel Shift?

____
____
____
____
____
____

54/68

Date ____________________

Score ____________________

Language Arts 903 Alternate Test

Name ______________________________

Add the diacritical markings to the following words; then spell the words correctly (diacritical marks, 1 point; correct spelling, 1 point).

1. mung grul ______________________________
2. I pit u me ______________________________
3. vej u tu bul ______________________________
4. fer lo ______________________________
5. hik up ______________________________

Spell these words correctly (each answer, 2 points).

6. kal′ vur ē ______________________________
7. stär ______________________________
8. glãr ______________________________
9. lēs ______________________________
10. rēd ______________________________
11. u lärm′ ______________________________
12. mēt ______________________________
13. lā′ ur ______________________________
14. dē′ mun ______________________________
15. myüz ______________________________

Write the letter of the correct definition on each line (each answer, 2 points).

16. canny ______
    a. indifferent
    b. shrewd
    c. wild
    d. stupid
17. tranquil ______
    a. peaceful
    b. erratic
    c. sullen
    d. angry
18. entice ______
    a. drag
    b. employ
    c. tempt
    d. destroy
19. nonchalant ______
    a. excited
    b. indifferent
    c. radical
    d. testy
20. pugnacious ______
    a. thrifty
    b. dumb
    c. inadequate
    d. fond of fighting
21. morbid ______
    a. sickly
    b. grand
    c. repentant
    d. thoughtful

22. confront ______
    a. hide carefully
    b. speak softly
    c. face boldly
    d. avoid deliberately
23. gaunt ______
    a. healthy
    b. talented
    c. fat
    d. thin
24. alloy ______
    a. business partner
    b. alcoholic beverage
    c. metallic mixture
    d. military foe
25. fickle ______
    a. sickly
    b. changeable
    c. unwanted
    d. steady

Write *C* by the correctly spelled words and correct the misspelled words (each answer, 1 point).

26. busines ________________
27. critycal ________________
28. absolutely ________________
29. uncertain ________________
30. stupidety ________________
31. arrest ________________
32. composition ________________
33. aquarium ________________
34. cumunication ________________
35. beliefe ________________

Write one correctly spelled word for each mnemonic (each answer, 2 points).

36. careful pronunciation ________________
37. rent ________________
38. exaggerated pronunciation ________________
39. current event ________________
40. When in doubt, use *-or* ________________

Make the following outline parallel (this numbered item, 5 points).

41. I. The Origin of Peace
    - A. True peace is oneness — a. ________________
    - B. The secret of oneness — b. ________________

    II. The Process of Peace
    - A. Christ and the middle wall of hostility — c. ________________
    - B. A whole new man — d. ________________

    III. You need to possess peace — e. ________________
    - A. God has given a message to believe
    - B. Jesus has opened the way to communication

Read this lead sentence and answer the questions (each answer, 1 point).

The commander of Williams Air Force Base said Wednesday that he fears construction of homes within a "potential crash zone" will start if a state moratorium banning building near air force bases is lifted.

42. Who? ________________
43. What? ________________
44. When? ________________
45. Where? ________________
46. Why? ________________

Complete this list (each answer, 1 point).

47. The usual three-part advice given to public speakers is a. ________________, b. ________________, and c. ________________.

66/83

Date ________________
Score ________________

Name ____________________

Match these items (each answer, 2 points).

1. _______ topic
2. _______ topic sentence
3. _______ main idea
4. _______ supporting detail
5. _______ generalization
6. _______ compare
7. _______ contrast
8. _______ imagery
9. _______ diction
10. _______ narrator

a. comparing only differences in things
b. one who tells a story
c. spatial order
d. choice of words
e. sentence stating main idea
f. figurative language evoking mental pictures
g. subject for discussion
h. most important part of a paragraph
i. putting together all the information to form an overall picture
j. emphasizing the differences and similarities of things
k. a sentence explaining or proving the main idea

Write the letter for the correct answer on each line (each answer, 2 points).

11. A character who does not change in the course of the story is a ____________ character.
    a. flat c. round
    b. static d. dynamic
12. The world in which the characters of a story move is its ____________.
    a. conflict c. atmosphere
    b. imagery d. diction
13. The observation an author makes about life in his story is its ________.
    a. theme c. conflict
    b. plot d. characters
14. A paragraph whose topic sentence comes in mid-paragraph is said to have a ____________ shape.
    a. triangle c. square
    b. rectangle d. diamond
15. The pattern of incidents making up a story is its ______________.
    a. plot c. diction
    b. setting d. theme
16. A complex character with many traits is a ______________ character.
    a. flat c. real
    b. round d. concrete

17. The physical and sometimes moral background against which a story takes place is the ______________.
    a. plot c. setting
    b. moral d. theme
18. When an author uses something that stands for or represents something else, that something becomes ______________.
    a. plot c. an idea
    b. character d. a symbol
19. When a theme is present but not stated directly by the author, that theme is said to be ______________.
    a. implied c. illustrated
    b. pictured d. absent
20. Both Herman Melville and Nathaniel Hawthorne used ______________ to give added meaning to their work.
    a. plot c. atmosphere
    b. symbolism d. conflict

Complete these statements (each answer, 3 points).

21. A character who is both unique and a representative of all mankind is a ________________________ type.
22. The two basic parts of every paragraph are the a. __________________ and the b. ________________________.
23. Chronological order deals with the ordering of __________________.
24. Creating imaginary people who seem real is the art of ______________.

Write *true* or *false* (each answer, 1 point).

25. _______ A round character can be static or dynamic.
26. _______ The theme of a short story must be directly stated in the work.
27. _______ Spatial order is most often used for description.
28. _______ The atmosphere of a story is created by the author's diction, sentence structure, and style.
29. _______ The foundation of any short story is character.

Date ____________________
Score ____________________

Name ______________________

Match these items (each answer, 2 points).

1. _______ poetry
2. _______ Dickens
3. _______ short story
4. _______ gerund
5. _______ tragedy
6. _______ participle
7. _______ "I don't never study"
8. _______ climax
9. _______ denouement
10. _______ soliloquy

a. a solo speech given by a character
b. a verb form ending in *-ing* and used as an adjective
c. double negative
d. the exciting part of the story
e. important for developing characters
f. literary form relying on sound and rhythm
g a nonliteral meaning used to describe things
h. first developed by American authors
i. a verb form ending in *-ing* and used as a noun
j. characterized by pathos and sorrow
k. the resolution of the story's action

Complete these statements (each answer, 3 points).

11. The term describing a literary type, such as the novel or short story, is ____________________.
12. The character working for good in a novel, drama, or short story is the ____________________.
13. The character working against good is called the ____________________.
14. When an adjective or an adverb in the comparative or superlative degree ending in (*-er* or *-est*) is compared again in the analytical form, the result is an error called ____________________.
15. In American English a collective noun takes ____________________ verbs and pronouns.
16. "Not never" is an example of a ____________________.
17. In the sentence, "preaching is Parson Brown's favorite activity," *preaching* is used as a/an a. ____________________ and is therefore a/an b. ____________________.
18. The phrase, "The most prettiest," is an example of a ____________________ ____________________.
19. In the sentence, "Singing the anthem beautifully, the sanctuary choir touched the emotions of the congregation," *singing* is used as a/an a. ____________________ and is therefore a/an b. ____________________.
20. The sentence, "He won't never go to church," is an example of the grammatical error called a. ____________________.

Write the missing comparative forms (each answer, 2 points).

21. holy a. __________ b. __________
22. a. __________ b. __________ best
23. bad a. __________ b. __________

Write the missing principal parts (each answer, 3 points).

24. lie a. __________ b. __________
25. think a. __________ b. __________
26. a. __________ b. __________ gone

Write the correct form of the word on each line (each answer, 2 points).

27. a. ______ (Is/Are) the freshman class ready with b. __________________ (its/it's/their/there) report?
28. The minister ______________________ (to bring (past tense)) comfort to the bereaved family.
29. The team a. ________________ (has/have) finished b. __________________ (its/it's/their/there) game.
30. One of the ________________________ (most sacred/most sacredest) privileges of a Christian is the participation in Communion, the Lord's Supper.

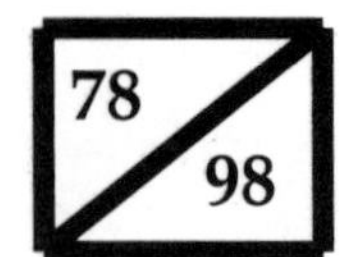

Date ______________________

Score ______________________

Name ______________________

Match these items (each answer, 2 points).

1. _______ metaphor
2. _______ statistics
3. _______ simile
4. _______ tetrameter
5. _______ straw man fallacy
6. _______ endorsement
7. _______ bandwagon approach
8. _______ pentameter
9. _______ chronological
10. _______ stanza

a. four or more lines of poetry: a verse "paragraph"
b. arranged in the order in which events occurred
c. a propagandistic technique using misleading arguments
d. the act of sanctioning a concept or product
e. five feet per line of poetry
f. factual data, numerical facts
g. movement with a regular beat
h. direct comparison; a figure of speech
i. implied comparison; figure of speech
j. "everybody's doing it" technique of propaganda
k. four feet per line of poetry

Complete these statements (each answer, 3 points).

11. Three sequence arrangements a reader should be able to identify are a.______________ order, b.______________ order, and order of importance.
12. Poetry is a special kind of music, using sound and______________ of words to create a musical quality.
13. Objective writing depends upon______________ rather than emotion.
14. One propaganda technique, narrowing all alternatives to two, is called the______________ fallacy.
15. Four kinds of graphs are a.______________, b.______________, c.______________, and d.______________.

16. Poems that rhyme at the end of the lines are said to have a__________ __________, such as *abba cdcd*.
17. A poetic foot comprised of two beats, an unstressed beat followed by a stressed one (ta-*tum*) is called a/an__________ foot.
18. A poetic foot comprised of two beats, a stressed one followed by an unstressed one (*tum*- ta) is called a/an__________ foot.
19. Unrhymed iambic pentameter poetry is called__________.
20. Some poetry, such as Poe's "The Raven," tells a story and is called __________ verse or poetry.

Answer *true* or *false* (each answer, 1 point).

21. ______ Emotionally-charged words encourage fear, panic, hatred, loyalty, love, devotion, and pride.
22. ______ Endorsements may be used in politics, evangelism, and promotions for the arts, as well as in advertising.
23. ______ A fallacy uses a truthful and accurate statement.
24. ______ To be a critical reader, you need to be able to identify both the stated and the implied purposes.
25. ______ A biography would use spatial order.

Study the chart and answer the following questions (each answer, 2 points).

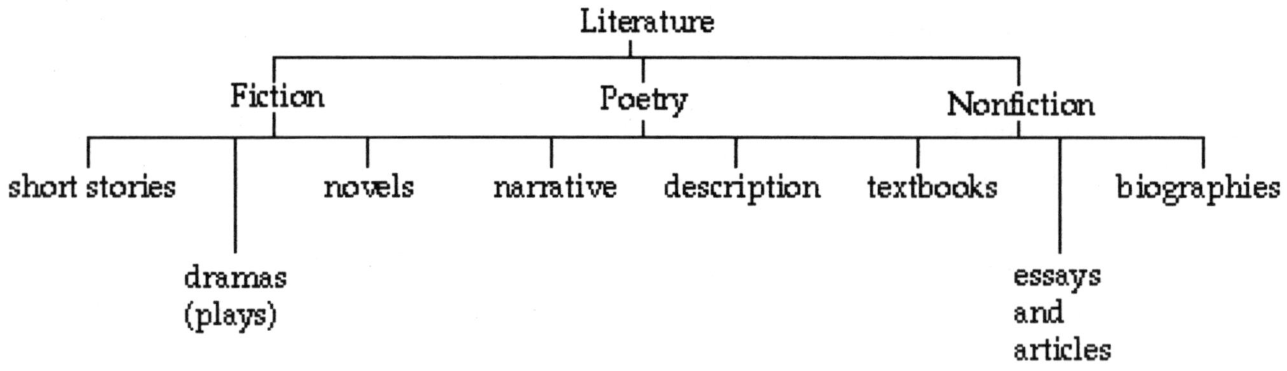

Literature
- Fiction
  - short stories
  - dramas (plays)
  - novels
- Poetry
  - narrative
  - description
- Nonfiction
  - textbooks
  - essays and articles
  - biographies

26. How many kinds of fiction are there? __________
27. Would a newspaper article be classified as fiction, poetry, or non-fiction? __________
28. What kind of literature is a play? __________

29. What are the three main divisions of literature?

 a.________________ b.________________ c.__________________

30. To what main category (genre) would a LIFEPAC belong? __________

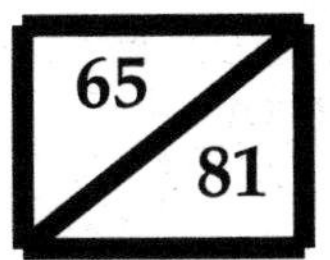

Date ______________________________________
Score ______________________________________

Name ______________________

Write *true* or *false* (each answer, 1 point).

1. _______ The three essential qualities of a speaker are sincerity, friendliness, and authority.
2. _______ The ABC's of good business letters include accuracy, brevity, and courage.
3. _______ Nervous energy generated by an opportunity to speak in public cannot be utilized to make you a better speaker.
4. _______ A speech is simply an expansion of thoughtful, friendly conversation between two people.
5. _______ A properly written business letter serves as a record of a proposal or a transaction.
6. _______ If you apologize at the beginning of your speech, you are suggesting to the audience that you have a poor evaluation of yourself and your work.
7. _______ An example of an internal condition affecting listening is loud music or noise from another classroom.
8. _______ Do not include a joke in your speech unless it really illustrates a point you wish to make.
9. _______ The most important thing to do in planning a speech is to decide on the central idea and form it into a sentence.
10. _______ Voice variety—high notes, low notes, emotional tones, and intellectual overtones—produces expressiveness and may be produced by thinking the appropriate expression.

Match these items (each answer, 2 points).

11. _______ salutation
12. _______ voice quality
13. _______ larynx
14. _______ listening
15. _______ tympanic membrane
16. _______ proofreading
17. _______ cochlea
18. _______ trite
19. _______ acoustics
20. _______ indelible

a. the eardrum
b. checking for grammatical, spelling, and typographical errors
c. greeting
d. worn out
e. structural features of an auditorium
f. cannot be removed or washed out
g. paying active attention to the words of a speaker
h. the malleus
i. result of length, size, tension, and elasticity of the vocal cords together with breath pressure
j. spiral tube of the inner ear that contains nerve endings
k. the "voice box"

Complete these sentences (each answer, 3 points).

21. Good conversation depends upon good ____________________ as well as skillful, interesting speaking.
22. An informal or "friendly" letter is usually written in ____________________ English.
23. Three voice qualities are a.__________________, b.__________________ and c.__________________.
24. A letter written to comfort someone who has experienced a personal sorrow is called a letter of consolation or__________________.
25. The resonators, which include the throat, the mouth, and the ______________ __________________, amplify tone, determine the degree of nasality, and generally determine the basic quality of a person's voice.
26. Three principles of a good conversationalist are a. __________________, b.__________________, and c.__________________.
27. Reading back over a letter or a paper to check for content, spelling, punctuation, and grammar is called__________________.
28. Three outer distractions to good listening are a.__________________, b.__________________, and c.__________________.
29. Three parts of a business letter are the a.__________________, b.__________________, and c.__________________.
30. The other three parts of a business letter include the a.__________________, b.__________________, and c.__________________.

72/90

Date ____________________
Score ____________________

Name ____________________

Match these items (each answer, 2 points).

1. ______ stage direction
2. ______ life history
3. ______ obedience
4. ______ exposition
5. ______ listing of sources
6. ______ climax
7. ______ complication
8. ______ memoirs
9. ______ denouement
10. ______ Renaissance

a. shows entanglement of characters, motive
b. introduces theme and characters
c. solution
d. biography
e. the revival of learning
f. autobiography
g. prose suggesting characters' movements and motives
h. the "turning point" of action
i. "gateway" to learning
j. a static character
k. bibliography

Complete these statements (each answer, 3 points).

11. The *Readers' Guide* indexes about 165 popular______________ .
12. The etymology, or ______________ of a word, may be found in the *Oxford English Dictionary.*
13. You may find a book in the card catalog if you know one of the following items: a.__________ , b.__________ , or c.__________ .
14. You may use the__________to locate an item in a newspaper.
15. Two systems of classifying books in the library includes the a.__________ and the b.__________systems.
16. A dictionary of synonyms and antonyms is a/an__________ .
17. The identifying number of a book, found on its spine or in the upper left corner of a card in the catalog, is its ______________________ number.

Write the letter for the correct answer on each line (each answer, 2 points).

18. Most historians agree that drama probably evolved from religious ceremonies in ____________ .
    a. Greece
    b. England
    c. Italy
    d. Germany
19. The author of *The Miracle Worker* is ____________ .
    a. Ben Jonson
    b. Arthur Millerd.
    c. William Gibson
    d. Thornton Wilder
20. The best choice of a dictionary to use in discovering the etymology of a word is ____________ .
    a. *Collegiate Dictionary*
    b. *Oxford English Dictionary*
    c. *Dictionary of American Biography*
    d. *Roget's Thesaurus*
21. Helen's associating the word *water* with the substance "water" marks the ____________ of the play.
    a. exposition
    b. climax
    c. denouement
    d. conflict
22. To find a magazine article about William Shakespeare, you would look in the ____________ .
    a. encyclopedia
    b. card catalog
    c. *Readers' Guide*
    d. vertical file

Answer these questions (each answer, 5 points).

23. How should you choose an encyclopedia best suited for your purposes?
    ____
    ____
    ____
24. Briefly, what is the historical development of drama?
    ____
    ____
    ____

56/70

Date ____________
Score ____________

Answer *true* or *false* (each answer, 1 point).

1. _______ The term *novel* can be defined as a long prose narrative.
2. _______ The term *romance* comes from the word *novella.*
3. _______ The dominant idea of a novel is its plot.
4. _______ The novel is a product of the eighteenth century.
5. _______ A pastoral poem is written about shepherds and rural life.
6. _______ A didactic novel is entertaining not instructive.
7. _______ There is basically only one type of novel.
8. _______ A naturalistic novel has a pessimistic outlook.
9. _______ Realism is a highly personal way of writing.
10. _______ William Dean Howells called realism "the truthful treatment of material."

Match these items (each answer, 2 points)

11.	_______	Jules Verne	a.	*Troilus and Criseyde*
12.	_______	denouement	b.	example of a novel of incidence
13.	_______	caricature	c.	James Boswell
14.	_______	naturalism	d.	*Journey to the Center of the Earth*
15.	_______	narrative	e.	the true story of an individual life
16.	_______	Geoffrey Chaucer	f.	the resolving of the action
17.	_______	Leo Tolstoy	g.	an extreme, unbelievable character
18.	_______	Robinson Crusoe	h.	a story or account
19.	_______	biography	i.	*War and Peace*
20.	_______	*Life of Johnson*	j.	based on determinism

Write the letter for the correct answer on each line (each answer, 2 points).

21. All plots must have ______________.
    a. themes
    b. conflicts
    c. action
    d. dialogue

22. A character who changes during the course of the story is ______________.
    a. flat
    b. round
    c. static
    d. dynamic

23. The method that answers the question, "How does the writer say it?" is ______________.
    a. analysis
    b. evaluation
    c. interpretation
    d. summary

24. The critical method that determines whether an author's statement is worthwhile is ______________.
    a. evaluation
    b. analysis
    c. interpretation
    d. paraphrasing

25. The root word *criticism* is ______________.
    a. English
    b. Latin
    c. Greek
    d. Celtic

26. To give the meaning of someone else's writing in your words is ______________.
    a. evaluating
    b. paraphrasing
    c. summarizing
    d. repeating

27. The first step in writing an essay is to ______________.
    a. find evidence
    b. make an outline
    c. select a topic
    d. know your text

28. A thesis must be supported by ______________.
    a. evidence
    b. outlines
    c. paragraphs
    d. other novels

29. To make clear the meaning of a work of literature is to ______________ it.
    a. analyze
    b. criticize
    c. ascertain
    d. explicate

30. Jane Austen's *Pride and Prejudice* is an example of a ______________.
    a. gothic novel
    b. novel of manners
    c. historical novel
    d. romance

Complete these statements (each answer, 3 points).

31. A character that changes little or not at all is a ________________ character.
32. The five most common modes of writing a novel are a.________________ b.________________, c. ________________ d. ________________, and e.________________.
33. The most famous example of the method of expressionism is James Joyce's ________________.
34. The gothic form of the novel contains the ingredients of a. ________________ and b. ________________.
35. The author who gave us the historical novel was ________________.
36. The first clear and fully developed novel was a. ________________ by b. ________________.
37. Science fiction is really a work of ________________.
38. Three of the seven types of novels defined in this study include a. ________________, b. ________________, and c. ________________.
39. The core of a realistic novel is ________________.
40. The point of view of the narrator in *Twenty Thousand Leagues under the Sea* is ________________.

38. Three of the seven types of novels defined in this study include a. ________________, b.________________, and c.________________.
39. The core of a realistic novel is ________________.
40. The point of view of the narrator in *Twenty Thousand Leagues under the Sea* is ________________.

83/104

Date ________________
Score ________________

Answer *true* or *false* (each answer, 1 point).

1. _______ A comparison using *like* or *as* is called a simile.
2. _______ Half of our English words derive from Germanic origin.
3. _______ *To run* is an example of a gerund.
4. _______ The tympanic membrane is a spiral tube in the inner ear that contains nerves.
5. _______ English is a Germanic language.
6. _______ All poetry must rhyme.
7. _______ Chaucer wrote in Middle English.
8. _______ A library computer or card catalog lists authors by subject, title, and book.
9. _______ Most poetry relies upon implied meaning.
10. _______ *Tree* is an abstract noun.

Match these items (each answer, 2 points).

11. _______ Gaelic
12. _______ fallacy
13. _______ participle
14 _______ topic sentence
15. _______ denouement
16. _______ infinitive
17. _______ conflict
18. _______ gerund
19. _______ thesis
20. _______ slant rhyme

a. main idea of a paragraph
b. *sing* and *think*
c. the "problem" of the story
d. a Celtic language
e. *singing* used as an adjective
f. main idea of an entire paper or speech
g. a direct comparison
h. conclusion of the story or drama
i. a faulty argument
j. *to sing*
k. *singing* used as a noun

Complete these statements (each answer, 3 points).

21. Three kinds of letters include a.________________ , b.________________ and c.________________ .

22. The best reference tool to help you find a book in the library would be a.________________ ; to find a magazine article, b.________________ and to find general information, c.________________ .

Write the correct word or words from the sentence in the appropriate places on the sentence diagram. Note that not all parts of the sentence will be diagrammed for this exercise (each answer, 2 points).

23. The minister from California chose a verse from Second Corinthians as the text for the sermon.

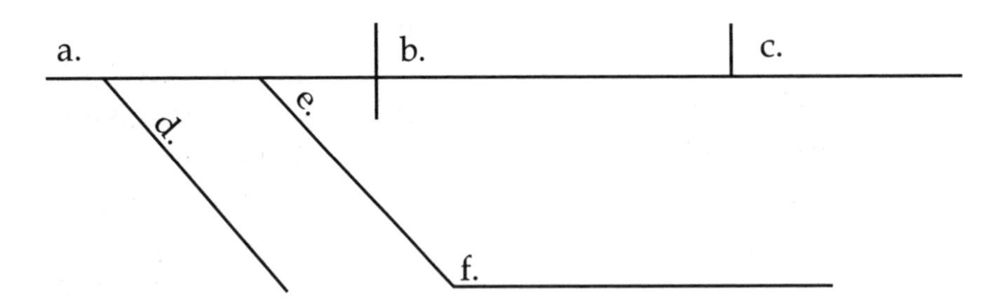

48 / 60

Date ________________

Score ________________

1. true
2. false
3. true
4. false
5. true
6. true
7. false
8. true
9. true
10. true
11. m
12. d
13. a
14. h
15. b
16. i
17. j
18. k
19. c
20. l
21. e
22. f
23. indicative
24. Either order:
    a. adjective
    b. adverb
25. infinitive phrase
26. appositive
27. complex
28. part of speech
29. complete predicate
30. direct object
31. complement
32. collective
33. b
34. a
35. c
36. a
37. d
38. c

39.

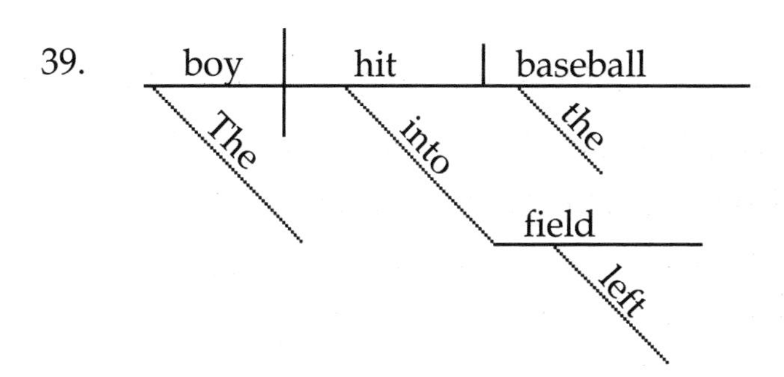

40.

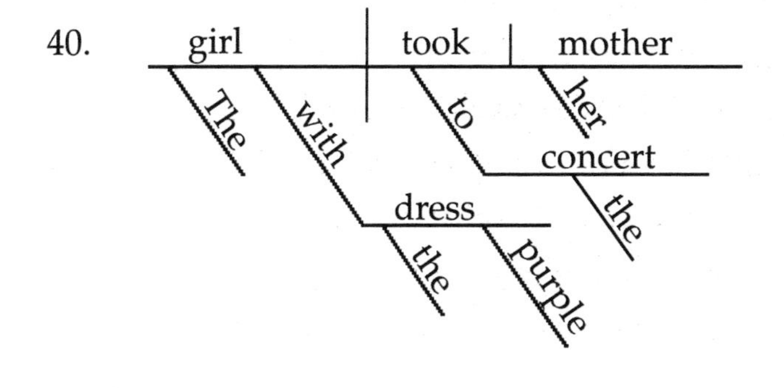

1. f
2. g
3. e
4. a
5. c
6. b
7. true
8. false
9. true
10. true
11. true
12. b
13. a
14. c
15. d
16. b
17. c
18. b
19. a
20. b
21. c
22. b
23. Either order:
    a. Greek
    b. Hebrew
24. special
25. plan
26. Babel
27. Latin
28. root
29. Old English
30. Example: Until Chaucer's time an effort had been made to keep the vowels "pure," both in speaking and in writing. Pure vowels do not have a diphthongal glide as we have in our long vowels today. This glide was taking place in Anglo-Saxon speech at that time and writers were having trouble spelling these sounds.

1. mun′ grul - mongrel
2. i pit′ u mē - epitome
3. vej′ u tu bul - vegetable
4. fėr′ lō - furlough
5. hik′ up - hiccup
6. calvary
7. star
8. glare
9. lease
10. read
11. alarm
12. meet or meat
13. layer
14. demon
15. muse
16. b
17. a
18. c
19. b
20. d
21. a
22. c
23. d
24. c
25. b
26. business
27. critical
28. C
29. C
30. stupidity
31. C
32. C
33. C
34. communication
35. belief

36-40 Examples:

36. library
37. superintendent
38. usually
39. occurrence
40. supervisor
41. Examples:
    a. True peace is oneness with Christ.
    b. The secret of oneness is a person.
    c. Christ has broken down the middle wall of hostility.
    d. Christ has made of two a whole new man
    e. The Possessing of Peace
42. the commander
43. fears destruction of homes
44. Wednesday
45. Williams Air Force Base
46. a state building moratorium is being lifted
47. a. tell them what you are going to tell them
    b. then tell them
    c. tell them what you have told them

Language Arts 904 Alternate Test Key

1. g
2. e
3. h
4. k
5. i
6. j
7. a
8. f
9. d
10. b
11. b
12. c
13. a
14. d
15. a
16. b
17. c
18. d
19. a
20. b
21. concrete-universal
22. Either order:
    a. main idea
    b. supporting details
23. time
24. characterization
25. true
26. false
27. true
28. true
29. false

1. f
2. e
3. h
4. i
5. j
6. b
7. c
8. d
9. k
10. a
11. genre
12. protagonist
13. antagonist
14. a double comparison
15. singular
16. double negative
17. a. noun
    b. gerund
18. double comparison
19. a. adjective
    b. participle
20. double negative
21. a. holier
    b. holiest
22. a. good
    b. better
23. a. worse
    b. worst
24. a. lay
    b. lain
25. a. thought
    b. thought
26. a. go
    b. went
27. a. Is
    b. its
28. brought
29. a. has
    b. its
30. most sacred

1. i
2. f
3. h
4. k
5. c
6. d
7. j
8. e
9. b
10. a
11. Either order:
    a. chronological
    b. spatial
12. rhythm
13. logic
14. either-or
15. Any order:
    a. bar
    b. line
    c. pictographs
    d. pie
16. rhyme scheme
17. iambic
18. trochaic
19. blank verse
20. narrative
21. true
22. true
23. false
24. true
25. false
26. three
27. nonfiction
28. drama or fiction
29. Any order:
    a. fiction
    b. poetry
    c. nonfiction
30. nonfiction

1. true
2. false
3. false
4. true
5. true
6. true
7. false
8. true
9. true
10. true
11. c
12. i
13. k
14. g
15. a
16. b
17. j
18. d
19. e
20. f
21. listening
22. colloquial
23. Any order:
    a. purity
    b. flexibility
    c. strength
24. condolence
25. nasal passages
26. Any order:
    a. that he is interested/relaxed
    b. that he is friendly/cheerful
    c. that he is courteous/tactful
27. proofreading
28. Any order:
    a. loud music or noise
    b. write on blackboard
    c. uncomfortable chair or too hot or cold room
29. Any order:
    a. heading
    b. inside address
    c. salutation or body, closing, signature
30. Any order:
    a. body
    b. closing
    c. signature or heading, inside address, salutation

1. g
2. d
3. i
4. b
5. k
6. h
7. a
8. f
9. c
10. e
11. periodicals (magazines)
12. history or development
13. Any order:
    a. author
    b. title
    c. subject
14. *New York Times Index*
15. Any order:
    a. Dewey Decimal
    b. Library of Congress
16. thesaurus
17. call
18. a
19 c
20. b
21. b
22. c
23. Example:
    General encyclopedias Summarize subjects, giving an overview of a topic. More detailed information can be found in specialized encyclopedias on art, religion, and so forth. Other sources should be consulted for further research.
24. Example:
    Drama developed from early religious ceremonies in Greece. Rome developed forms of drama until its decline. The ninth-century Christian church rituals fostered the development of mystery, miracle, and morality plays. During the Renaissance, Shakespeare and other playwrights produced outstanding works. The twentieth century has combined old traditions with new ideas and experimentation.

1. true
2. false
3. false
4. true
5. true
6. false
7. false
8. true
9. false
10. true
11. d
12. f
13. g
14. j
15. h
16. a
17. i
18. b
19. e
20. c
21. b
22. d
23. a
24. a
25. c
26. b
27. d
28. a
29. d
30. b
31. static
32. Any order:
    a. realism
    b. naturalism
    c. romanticism
    d. impressionism
    e. expressionism
33. *Finnegan's Wake*
34. Either order:
    a. magic
    b. mystery
35. Sir Walter Scott
36. a. *Pamela*
    b. Samuel Richardson
37. fantasy
38. Any order:
    a. gothic novel
    b. novel of manners
    c. historical novel
    or detective novel,
    psychological novel,
    problem novel, or
    regional novel
39. character or
    characterization
40. first person limited

1. true
2. false
3. false
4. false
5. true
6. false
7. true
8. false
9. true
10. false
11. d
12. i
13. e
14. f
15. h
16. j
17. c
18. k
19. f
20. b
21. Any order:
    a. informal
    b. social
    c. business
22. a. card catalog
    b. *Readers' Guide*
    c. encyclopedia
23. a. minister
    b. chose
    c. verse
    d. The
    e. from
    f. California

LIFEPAC

ANSWER KEYS

SECTION ONE

1.1 sentence
1.2 naming
1.3 tools
1.4 proper
1.5 capital
1.6 2 a. Desert flowers are beautiful in the spring.
1.7 4 b. His journey through space took him over both Africa and South America.
1.8 1 b. The first college in the United States was Harvard College.
1.9 5 a King John of England signed the Magna Charta in 1215.
1.10 10 b. The entire Bible is a message about Jesus Christ.
1.11 a
1.12 c
1.13 b
1.14 c
1.15 d
1.16 syllables
1.17 brushes
1.18 reports
1.19 adding - s
1.20 dresses
1.21 taxes
1.22 buzzes
1.23 peaches
1.24 adding -es
1.25 rodeos
1.26 studios
1.27 trios
1.28 adding - s
1.29 heroes
1.30 pianos (exception to rule)
1.31 tomatoes
1.32 adding - es
1.33 monkeys
1.34 toys
1.35 valleys
1.36 adding - s
1.37 allies
1.38 cities
1.39 changing y to i and adding - es
1.40 lives
1.41 beliefs
1.42 by adding - s or by changing f (fe) to v and adding - es
1.43 children
1.44 men

1.45 changing the spelling of the singular
1.46 fathers-in-law
1.47 post offices
1.48 adding the appropriate plural sign (-s or -es) to the main word
1.49 cupfuls
1.50 chalkboards
1.51 railways
1.52 adding the appropriate plural sign (-s or -es) to the end
1.53 -1.62 Examples:
1.53 a. (S) She is an alumna of Iowa State University.
b. (P) The alumnae are having a fund-raising dinner.
1.54 a. (S) The basis of their friendship was a common interest in travel.
b. (P) The bases for salvation rest upon Jesus' offering of forgiveness and a person's acceptance of His offer.
1.55 a. (S) A cell needs the nucleus in order to grow and divide into other cells.
b. (P) Nuclei of cells are located in different positions in different kind of cells.
1.56 a. (S) A series of rainy days spoiled the camping trip.
b. (P) The ball games which are played in the World Series are of interest to many people.
1.57 a. (S) (This noun appears only in the plural form.)
b. (P) He sharpened all the scissors in the schoolroom.
1.58 a. (S) A study of civics is helpful in preparing a student for life as an adult.
b. (P) (This noun has singular meaning and takes a singular verb.)
1.59 a. (S) Quick thinking is the means by which trouble is often avoided.
b. (P) What are the means by which you are going to solve the problems?
1.60 a. (S) (This noun appears only in the plural form.)
b. (P) All the riches in the world cannot buy happiness.
1.61 a. (S) An analysis of the situation will help solve the problem.
b. (P) The experts prepared written analysis of the traffic problem.
1.62 a. (S) Athletics is recommended for high school students.
b. (P) (This noun has singular meaning and takes a singular verb.)
1.63 horse's
1.64 friend's
1.65 teacher's
1.66 dogs'
1.67 girls'
1.68 guests'
1.69 businessmen's
1.70 sisters-in-law's
1.71 Secretaries of State's
1.72 oxen's
1.73 Theresa's and Marylin's fathers
1.74 Milli and Mike's mother

1.75 -1.79 Examples:

1.75 Snoopy is my favorite comic-strip character.

1.76 A warm, humid breeze is blowing.

1.77 The beautiful girl is smiling.

1.78 The tree, green and slender, bent in the summer breeze.

1.79 The woman at the desk is competent.

Examples using suffixes as adjective endings:

enjoyable	peaceable
natural	ornamental
Asian	Hawaiian
assistant	buoyant
angular	circular
stationary	ordinary
literate	immaculate
broken	darken
different	excellent
joyful	useful
heroic	stoic
boyish	selfish
active	passive
helpless	toothless
loudly	quickly
famous	nervous
meddlesome	troublesome
sleepy	velvety

1.80 a

1.81 b

1.82 b

SECTION TWO

2.1 a. love b. loved

2.2 a. obeyed b. obeyed

2.3 a. brought b. brought

2.4 a. get b. got

2.5 a. swung b. swung

2.6 borne

2.7 beat

2.8 chose

2.9 sworn

2.10 tear

2.11 a. begin b. begun

2.12 a. swam b. swum

2.13 a. came b. come

2.14 a. eat b. eaten

2.15 a. ride b. rode

2.16 b

2.17 c

2.18 b

2.19 c

2.20 a

2.21 d

2.22 a

2.23 b

2.24 you have seen

2.25 he/she/it sees

2.26 I saw

2.27 you had seen

2.28 a. they saw
b. they had seen

2.29 we shall see

2.30 you will see

2.31 they will have seen

2.32 we have been seen

2.33 you are seen

2.34 he/she/it has been seen

2.35 I was seen

2.36 you had been seen

2.37 they were seen
2.38 I shall have been seen
2.39 you will be seen
2.40 they will have been seen
2.41 b
2.42 e
2.43 a
2.44 c
2.45 -2.48 Examples;
2.45 The dress is pink.
2.46 He jogs often.
2.47 He hit the ball.
2.48 The pie was eaten quickly by Jill.
2.49 Conjugation is a systematic arrangement of the forms of a verb according to tense, voice, mood, person, and number.
2.50 A transitive verb is a verb that has a receiver of the action named in the sentence.
2.51 lie
2.52 laid
2.53 sit
2.54 sat
2.55 rose
2.56 rise
2.57 true
2.58 false
2.59 false
2.60 true
2.61 best
2.62 better
2.63 smaller
2.64 most careful
2.65 older
2.66 Example:
The dog was not unfriendly.

SECTION THREE

3.1 her
3.2 They
3.3 them
3.4 We
3.5 his
3.6 Rel
3.7 Ind
3.8 Dem
3.9 Ind
3.10 Dem
3.11 Int
3.12 Rel
3.13 Int
3.14 its
3.15 his
3.16 his
3.17 her
3.18 their
3.19 his
3.20 her
3.21 The Grand Canyon is (<u>in</u> Arizona).
3.22 Kentucky bluegrass was brought (<u>to</u> America) (<u>from</u> Europe) .
3.23 The clock (<u>with</u> the luminous dial) can be seen (<u>in</u> the dark).
3.24 (<u>In</u> 1647) the first tax-supported schools were established (<u>by</u> law) (<u>in</u> the United States).
3.25 The first tax-supported schools (<u>in</u> the United States) taught boys and girls how to read the Bible.

3.26 (In 1963) the United States Supreme Court made required Bible reading illegal (in tax-supported schools).
3.27 The fear (of the Lord) is the beginning (of both knowledge and wisdom).
3.28 Reading the Bible is necessary (for Christian growth).
3.29 The Christian cannot grow spiritually (without regular Bible reading and prayer).
3.30 (With Bible reading and prayer) Christian fellowship and witnessing are also necessary principles (of Christian growth).
3.31 from
3.32 from
3.33 by
3.34 as
3.35 among
3.36 with
3.37 for
3.38 besides
3.39 into
3.40 on
3.41 correlative - Neither the sermon nor the song service was very long.
3.42 conjunctive adverb - We shall leave immediately; consequently, we shall arrive on time.
3.43 subordinating - We were not at home when our friends arrived.
3.44 co-ordinating - The teacher spoke quietly, but firmly.
3.45 correlative - Both the dictionary and the encyclopedia are valuable tools for study.
3.46 Hint:
An interjection is a word used to express sudden or strong feeling or emotion. Interjections are used for short exclamations.

SECTION FOUR

4.1-4.2 Examples:
4.1 a. The house (with the green shutters) is for sale.

b. The vegetables (in your garden) need to be watered.

4.2 a. The red coat was sent to me (by my aunt).

b. (At the end of the day), I go home.
4.3 gerund
(jogging early in the morning)
4.4 infinitive
(to speak effectively)
4.5 participial
(playing the piano)
4.6 gerund
(Crossing the street on a red light)
4.7 participial
(requiring much patience and skill)
4.8 infinitive
(To understand the other person's point of view)
4.9 gerund
(faithful witnessing)
4.10 participial
(Writing to the Thessalonians)
4.11 Examples:
a Mrs. Green, our science teacher, gave us an assignment.

b. Bill, the boy in the red shirt, is the captain of the football team.

4.12 noun
(What one believes)

4.13 adverb
(because He loved us)

4.14 adverb
(If we love one another)

4.15 noun
(What one does)

4.16 noun
(Whoever is born of God)

4.17 adjective
(who believes on the Son)

4.18 adverb
(If we confess our sins)

4.19 adjective
(who practices sin)

4.20 adjective
(who walketh not in the . . . .)

SECTION FIVE

5.1 p.n.
5.2 i.o.
5.3 d.o.
5.4 s.
5.5 p.
5.6 d.o.
5.7 d.o.
5.8 s.
5.9 p.a.
5.10 p.n.
5.11 d.o.
5.12 i.o.
5.13 p.
5.14 s.
5.15 p.a.

5.16

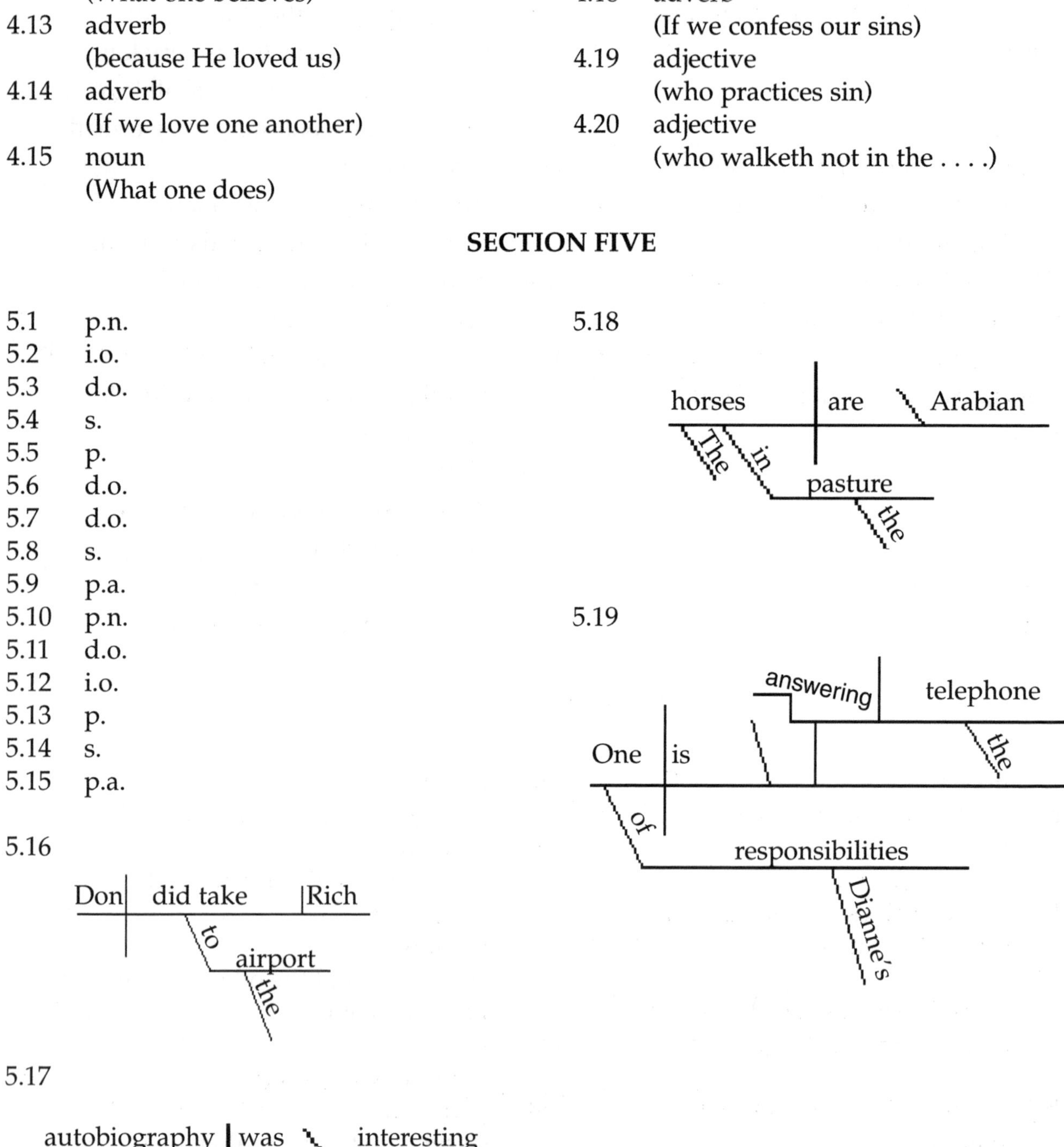

5.17

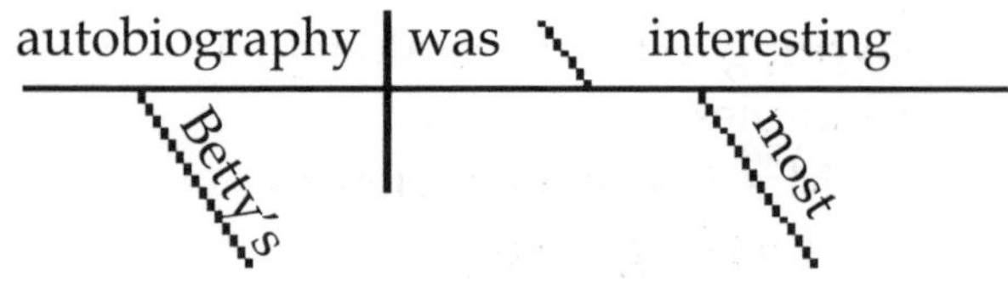

5.18

5.19

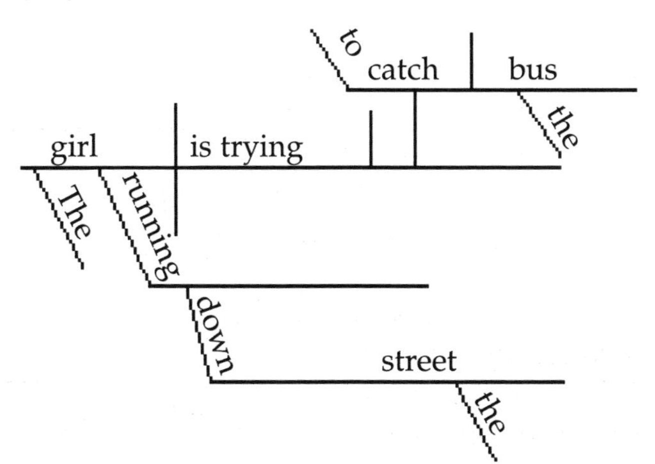

5.21

one
believes
What
determines
character
his

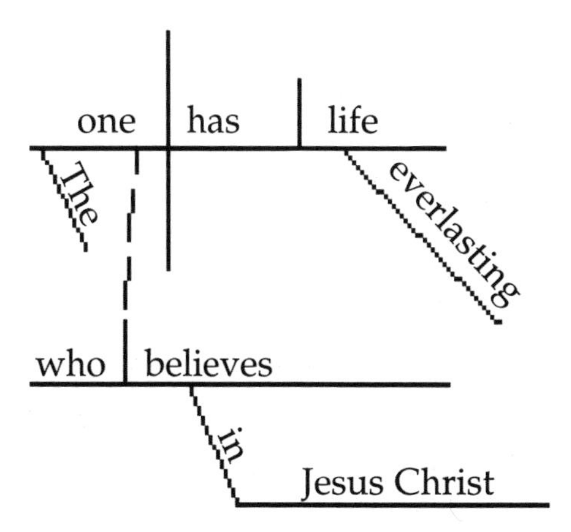

5.23

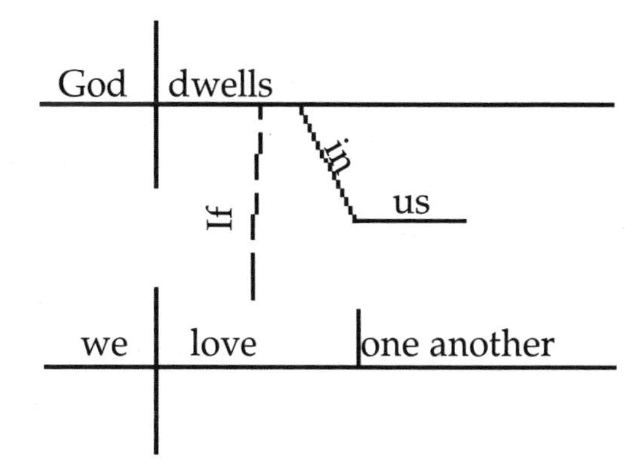

SECTION ONE

1.1 God
1.2 said
1.3 Abraham
1.4 Noah
1.5 nouns
1.6 j
1.7 b
1.8 d
1.9 g
1.10 e
1.11 f
1.12 c
1.13 i
1.14 h
1.15 a
1.16 Observations will vary.
1.17 Hint:
If you have told about the well-organized language before Abraham's time and have explained how perfectly Adam used language, you are on the right track.
1.18 Languages have in common a pattern of sounds, a collection of words, a system or word arrangement, and elements of grammar.
1.19 Either order:
a. Syntax. Syntax means meaningful order of words.
b. Morphology. Morphology is the variation of words to show how they serve in a sentence.
1.20 The different arrangement of words in one tongue is sometimes called the thought pattern of that tongue.
1.21 Hint:
You should have mentioned all four of the things common to all true language. Animals cannot acquire any of these because of physical and mental (their tongues, jaws, lungs, minds) limitations.
1.22 true
1.23 false
1.24 false
1.25 true
1.26 true
1.27 Dialogues will vary.

SECTION TWO

2.1 b
2.2 c
2.3 b
2.4 d
2.5 b
2.6 teacher check
2.7 In Genesis 11:4 the people are building the Tower of Babel to glorify themselves. They are trying to build it so that others will fear them and they will have power. God confounds their language so that they will realize He is necessary — that man's efforts are feeble without God.

2.8 Indo -European
2.9 Indus
2.10 Any order:
  a. French
  b. Spanish
  c. Portuguese
  d. Italian
  e. Romanian
2.11 Any order:
  a. Dutch-Flemish
  b. German
  c. English
  d. Norwegian
  e. Swedish
  f. Danish
  g. Icelandic
2.12 Greek
2.13 Any order:
  a. Gaelic
  b. Scots-Gaelic
  c. Welsh
  d. Breton
2.14 Breton (Briton)
2.15 Germanic — any order:
  1. Dutch-Flemish
  2. German
  3. English
  4. Norwegian
  5. Swedish
  6. Danish — Icelandic

  Latin — any order:
  1. Portuguese
  2. French
  3. Spanish
  4. Italian
  5. Romanian

  Greek — no languages

  Celtic — any order:
  1. Gaelic
  2. Scots-Gaelic
  3. Welsh
  4. Breton
2.16 false
2.17 true
2.18 false
2.19 true
2.20 true
2.21 true
2.22 false
2.23 false
2.24 true
2.25 true
2.26 Any order:
  a. Case — a form of noun, pronoun, or adjective.
  b. Mood— form of verb in English language.
  c. Number — singular of plural forms of words.
  d. Person — changes in nouns or verbs to show speaker.
  e. Tense— form of verb which shows time.
2.27 Hint:
  The dictionary will tell you the language from which many words are derived.
2.28

a	tea	e.	eggs
b.	bacon, toast	f.	butter
c.	coffee	g.	cereal
d.	marmalade	h.	cocoa

2.29 Pure vowels are vowels with a steady sound not a diphthongal glide as we have in our long vowels today.
2.30 The Great Vowel Shift was a gradual change in the pronunciation of all the long vowels. This change brought the long vowel sounds closer to their modern pronunciation. The shift also greatly affected the spelling of these vowels.

SECTION THREE

3.1 vocabulary

3.2 obsolete
3.3 citizenship (or manner of life)
3.4 queer (or strange)
3.5 corn
3.6 not having
3.7 spirit of a dead person
3.8 weak in mind
3.9 bashful, embarrassed
3.10 farmer
3.11 to allow
3.12 complete
3.13 giving to the poor

3.14 master of a household; husband
3.15 come after
3.16 Words will vary.

3.17 Words will vary.
3.18 "Why does your sword so drip with blood, Edward, Edward, Why does you sword so drip with blood?
And why do you walk so sadly, Oh?
"Oh, I have killed my hawk so good and I had no more but he, Oh."
"Your hawk's blood was never so red, Edward, Edward.
Your hawk's blood was never so red,
My dear son I tell thee, Oh."
"Oh, I have killed my red roan steed, Mother, Mother.
Oh, I have killed my red roan steed,
That once was so fair and free, Oh."

3.19-3.26 Answers will vary; examples are given:
3.19 sophisticated, sophomore
3.20 dialogue, logbook, logic
3.21 dissect, section, sectarian, sector, insect
3.22 autograph, biographical
3.23 plywood, implicit
3.24 indoctrinate, doctrine, document
3.25 tactile, tangible, tinged
3.26 manual, manage
3.27 does not
3.28 does not
3.29 illiterate — unable to read or write

3.30 encoded — locked in code form
3.31 irrelevant — does not apply
3.32 irresponsible — not someone to be depended upon

3.33 impatiently — not willing to wait

3.34 invincible — cannot be conquered
3.35 illogical — not making good sense or logic

3.36 illaudable — not worthy of praise

3.37 indoctrinate — to give teaching or instruction to another

3.38 irresistible — not able to stand against

3.39 a. able f. able
b. able g. able
c. able h. able
d. able i. able
e. able j. able

3.40 a. deplorable f. lovable
b. desirable g. sizable
c. debatable h. pleasurable
d. excitable i. usable
e. presumable j. valuable

3.41 a. enviable d. satisfiable
b. justifiable e. appreciable
c. reliable f. sociable

3.42 a. durable d. hospitable
b. irritable e. abominable
c. reparable f. penetrable

3.43 a. despicable e. applicable
b. educable f. amicable
c. emplacable g. practicable
d. revocable h. navigable

3.44 a. ible e. ible
b. ible f. ible
c. ible g. ible
d. ible h. ible

3.45 a. digestible c. exhaustible
b. corruptible d. contractible

3.46 a. ible d. ible
b. ible e. ible
c. ible f. ible

3.47 able II
3.48 able I
3.49 able I
3.50 ible VII
3.51 able V
3.52 ible VI
3.53 able I
3.54 ible VI
3.55 ible VIII
3.56 able III
3.57 able IV
3.58 able VIII (exception)

SECTION ONE

1.1 dis pik' u bul, des' pik u bul
1.2 u men' u tē, u mēn' u te
1.3 i ref' yü tu bul, ir' i fyü' tu bul

1.4 ek' skwi zit, ek skwiz' it

1.5 vej' tu bul, vej' u tu bul

1.6 picture, pitcher (circled: picture)
1.7 furnish, furnace (circled: furnish)

1.8 lawyer, layer (circled: lawyer)
1.9 comma, coma (circled: coma)

1.10 calvary, cavalry (circled: cavalry)

1.11 credible, credulous (circled: credible)
1.12 worst, worse (circled: worse)

1.13 preceded, proceeded (circled: proceeded)
1.14 furlong, furlough (circled: furlough)
1.15 temerity, timidity (circled: timidity)

1.16 f

1.17 j

1.18 h
1.19 e

1.20 a

1.21 l

1.22 k

1.23 c
1.24 d

1.25 b

1.26 c
1.27 a
1.28 b

1.29 a. yot
b. Example: J.P. Morgan once said that anyone who had to ask the price of a yacht couldn't afford one.

1.30 a. krō shā
b. Example:
I plan to crochet a cap for my sister's baby.

1.31 a kaz' um
b. Example:
He stood on the edge of the chasm looking into its depths.

1.32 a. hik' up
b. Example: None of the remedies helped his hiccoughs.

1.33 a. im pyun'
b. Example:
If you impugn my honesty, I will prove you wrong.

1.34 a. blag' ärd
b. Example:
Scotland Yard caught the blackguard hiding in a barn.

1.35 a. vit' ls
b. Example:
In return for ten hours of work per day, he was given a dollar a week, a room in the attic, and victuals.

1.36 a. in dīt'
b. Example:
Wilson's partner was also indicted, but he was found not guilty.

1.37 a. lar′ ingks
b. Example:
My friend injured his larynx in an accident and now he speaks in a whisper.

1.38 a. val′ id
b. Example:
Since the will was not signed, it was not valid.

SECTION TWO

2.1 Blind (blind)
were (where)
thay (they)
give (Give)
speach (speech)
deff (deaf)
thay (they)
give (Give)
knolage (knowledge)
strangth (strength)
exsperess (express)
themselfs (themselves)

2.2 Example:
Capitalize the first word in a sentence.

2.3 teacher check

2.4 teacher check

2.5 a. survivor, one who remains alive.
b. administrator, one who directs or manages.
c. spectator, one who looks on.
d. protector, one who defends from harm.
e. accelerator, that which increases speed.
f. fabricator, one who (or that which) puts things together.
g. prevaricator, one who tells lies.
h. visitor, one who calls on or stays with.
i. supervisor, one who oversees.
j. radiator, that which emits rays.
k. predecessor, one who goes before or has gone before.
l. commentator, one who comments, particularly on news.
m. investigator, one who inquires into.
n. indicator, that which signifies.
o. impostor, one who pretends to be someone else.
p. elevator, that which lifts up.
q. distributor, one who (or that which) allots.
r. educator, one who teaches.
s. aviator, one who flies a plane.

2.6 a. in′ fer ence
b. pref′ er ence
c. in cur′ rence
d. oc cur′ rence
e. ref′ er ence
f. trans′ fer ence (or trans fer′ ence)
g. de ter′ rence
h. re cur′ rence
i. con cur′ rence
j. ab hor′ rence
k. con′ fer ence
l. def′ er ence

2.7 a. dependence or dependance
b. attendance
c. reliance
d. difference
e. deliverance
f. assurance
g. repentance
h. utterance

2.8 false

2.9 false

2.10 true

2.11 true

2.12 false

SECTION THREE

3.1 neither
3.2 essay
3.3 essay
3.4 essay
3.5 report
3.6 report
3.7 neither
3.8 neither
3.9 essay
3.10 report
3.11 Example:
I. God made the world.
  A. God made the wonders of nature.
  B. God made plans for mankind to help build the world.
II. God made people
  A. God made the people I love.
  B. God made me.
III. God has acted in my life.
  A. God has been my guide.
  B. God has sent Christ to die for me.

3.12
Who? Jacobo Timerman
What? Was released and placed, etc.
Why? His cause was championed by many people
When? Monday
Where? Buenos Aires, Argentina

3.13 Lou Gehrig had unusual courage despite serious physical handicaps. ~~It rained about three times a week~~.
3.14 simple
3.15 simple
3.16 but, compound
3.17 but, compound
3.18 simple
3.19 simple
3.20 when I get home, complex
3.21 I never will go out for a walk, periodic
3.22 Example:
My little brother could not play outside because it was raining.
3.23 Example:
I will do my homework while you eat lunch.
3.24 Example:
I will eat rhubarb pie, although I really don't care for it.
3.25 teacher check

SECTION ONE

1.1 topic sentence
1.2 supporting details
1.3 friend's name
1.4 teacher check
1.5 ∆ Were it not for this relatively recent incident, the Parthenon would be standing intact today.
1.6 ∇ People say the necessities of life are food, water, shelter and clothing, but I think a fifth item should be added to the list: scotch tape.
1.7 ◇ Amnesia is, however, a very subtle and sometimes sinister illness.
1.8 teacher check
1.9 teacher check

1.10 a. □
b. Examples:
Lightning can strike trees, fire and radio towers, and skyscrapers.
1.11 a. ∆
b. The punch line, or main idea, always comes last.
1.12 a. ∆
b. A person is more likely to be receptive to new ideas if you begin your argument with things he can agree with. If you point out why your position is necessary then state your position, he is more likely to agree.
1.13 a. ∇
b. Example:
In a newspaper article the most important point should be stated first. The reader can then determine whether he is interested in reading more.
1.14 Hint:
Topic sentence should be the last sentence in the paragraph.
1.15 the last
1.16 You should have underlined first then, next, and last of all.
1.17 You should have underlined: surveyed, on the left, next to it, the back wall, and on its right.
1.18 a. Mom had to work late and the storm knocked out the electricity, so we had to eat cold cereal for supper.
b. It rained 5 inches in two hours; the streets were flooded, the electricity was out, the car wouldn't start , and I missed the party
c. About 100 years ago a man patented his invention for an incandescent bulb, starting thereby a new industry and signaling the demise of others.
d. We've all been in trouble since John and Tom started a fight in assembly.
1.19 Example:
so, since, because, as a result.
1.20 Being a good reader is somewhat like driving a car; both reader and driver must learn to shift gears skillfully. Just as road conditions that require slow, careful driving call for first gear, a difficult text requires slow, thoughtful reading to be understood and remembered. Similarly, the driver can shift to second gear if he wants to go slightly faster. Second gear is useful to a reader of textual material which is not difficult but which must be remembered. On the open road a driver shifts to third. Third gear in reading is used for pleasure reading of magazines or novels. Both readers and drivers sometimes use passing gear. This gear is particularly useful to a reader who wants to skim a chapter as a review for a test or to preview an article to determine whether he wishes to read it. Just

<u>as</u> driving in first gear at all times is inappropriate and inefficient, reading speeds must be shifted to suit conditions.

1.21 a. ∇ (first sentence underlined)
b. spatial order

1.22 a. ∇ (first sentence underlined)
b. Time order

1.23 a. ∇ (first sentence underlined)
b. comparison-contrast

1.24 a. ∇ (first sentence underlined)
b. spatial order

1.25 a. Δ (last sentence underlined)
b. cause-effect

1.26 b. Ravenna, Italy, is no longer an important city.

1.27 ▭

1.28 Example:
Alternate solutions to prison sentences for some convicts can benefit both the convict and society.

1.29 Hint:
Example of inverted triangle forms 1.25, 1.23, and 1.22.

1.30 <u>The contrast between these two settings is symbolic of the ultimate conflicts in Emily Bronte's novel *Wuthering Heights*</u>.

1.31 Δ

1.32 comparison/contrast

1.33 in sharp contrast

SECTION TWO

2.1 a. plot and setting
b. setting and characterization
c. theme and characterization

2.2 a. A man and his two sons
b. The younger son receives his inheritance, wastes it, gets a job feeding swine, and finally comes home to his father. His father forgives him and welcomes him. The older brother protests, but the father explains that the younger son was lost and is found.
c. a famine
d. Example:
A far country, fields, swine pens, the road to the father's home.
e. Example:
Those who have sinned and seek forgiveness should be forgiven.

2.3 Naomi is Ruth's mother-in-law.

2.4 a. She begs to be allowed to stay with Naomi and finally convinces her.
b. She cries and kisses her mother-in-law goodbye.
c. Ruth

2.5 Example:
a. Love of her mother-in-law, loyalty, obedience, humility
b. She is a generous, upright, godly person.

2.6 Her kinsman Boaz marries her so that she and Naomi will have descendants.

2.7 c

2.8 b

2.9 d

2.10 a

2.11 e

2.12 Example:
Virtue will be rewarded.

2.13 Example:
Author uses color words and specific detail.

2.14 Example:
Esther 1:6 Where were white, green, and blue, hangings, fastened with cords of fine linen and purple to silver rings and pillars of marble: the beds were of gold and silver, upon a pavement of red, and blue, and white, and black, ` marble.

2.15 Example:
Buds were swelling. The association

of youth and gladness with the rebirth symbolized by spring.

2.16 Example:
a mood of cheerfulness and gaiety

2.17 Example:
A mood of suspense and foreboding, as if something bad is about to happen.

2.18 They symbolize evil.

2.19 The name indicates youth, innocence and goodness. The commoness of the last name also indicates that the character is a concrete — universal character.

2.20 Example:
The serpent is another symbol of evil, as the snake in the Garden of Eden.

2.21 the devil

SECTION THREE

3.1 fall

3.2 ten miles

3.3 a sweater

3.4 He borrowed from a bank.

3.5 playing football

3.6 He did not have the money to pay back the bank

3.7 He and Grace collected ginseng, yellowroot, and May-apple root and sold it to Darby's store.

3.8 Example:
Grace had "ripe-wheat-colored hair". She was pretty. Students admired her for her high grades and her perseverance. She was loyal and sensitive to the feelings of others.

3.9 Jo-Anne was beautiful with dark hair — always "happy, laughing and showing her pretty teeth," but she was shallow — selfish, and insensitive to the feelings of others.

3.10 Grace would be his girl someday, but she would break up with Roy first gently, not tactlessly.

3.11 She really had me "hooked."
She held my love as firmly as the mountain loam held the roots of the wild flowers and the big trees.

3.12 She seemed very pretty.
she was as pretty as a cove sapling.

3.13 When the winter snows had begun to melt and the dogwood trees were in bloom.
as we were watching the blue melted

3.14 trickling below the ice.
singing its lonesome song beneath the ice

3.15 a. Example:
"And I knew she had the durability and toughness of storm - battered oak."

b. Example:
"Grace was as beautiful as our mountain was in April, prettier than a blossom of wild phlox or a mountain daisy."

3.16 Example:
People should not judge others by the way they look but by what they are.

3.17 Answers should include such points as: They walked 10 miles each day to and from school in all kinds of weather. Shan paid his way through school by hunting and trapping. Their fathers raised light Burley tobacco, a crop dependent on a good season; therefore luxuries were hard to come by.

3.18 teacher check

3.19 Example:
Charlie Gordon, a mentally retarded man, is given an operation which triples his I.Q. He keeps a detailed account of his progress, including scientific reports, but eventually his mind deteriorates and his I.Q. is back to 68.

3.20 A white rat that undergoes the same operation that Charlie does.

3.21 Example:
The flowers are symbolic of Charlies' empathy (identification) with Algernon.
3.22 The rat, Algernon
3.23 Example:
Charlie himself, his operation and perhaps the futility of the whole procedure.
3.24 Example:
If a person experiences an extreme, abrupt change in life, his old acquaintance and many of his friends could forsake him.
3.25 dynamic
3.26 His intelligence and his attitude change in response to the operation and his observations.
3.27 Example:
He learned that his friends had been laughing at him in his retarded condition. However, after experiencing the loneliness of being highly intelligent, he reaches out again to his old friends. Friends are very important.
3.28 teacher check

SECTION ONE

1.1 a. was
  b. its
1.2 meets
1.3 rises; applauds
1.4 Is
1.5 races
1.6 raises
1.7 a. opens
  b. its
1.8 community; gathers; crowd; family takes; agency; sells
1.9 Example: (teacher check)
  the press, the readership, defense, offense, team, batch, opposition, House, Senate, conference, staff, television
1.10 Example:
  In ordinary questions and statements in the present tense.
1.11 Example:
  Some end in -s or -ed without changing the spelling. Others change y to i and add -es or -ed. Some double the final consonant before adding -ed.

1.12 By adding -ing to the present indicative form (or to the verb stem).

1.13 a. marries
  b. marry
  b. married
  c. marrying

1.14 a. misses
  b. miss
  c. missed
  d. missing

1.15 a. mixes
  b. mix
  c. mixed
  d. mixing

1.16 a. moves
  b. move
  c. moved
  d. moving
1.17 a. occurs
  b. occur
  c. occurred
  d. occurring
1.18 a. plays
  b. play
  c. played
  d. playing
1.19 a. relies
  b rely
  c. relied
  d. relying
1.20 a. shouts
  b. shout
  c. shouted
  d. shouting
1.21 a. skates
  b. skate
  c. skated
  d. skating
1.22 a. skims
  b. skim
  c. skimmed
  d. skimming
1.23 a. sprays
  b. spray
  c. sprayed
  d. spraying
1.24 a. stays
  b. stay
  c. stayed
  d. staying
1.25 a. stops
  b. stop
  c. stopped
  d. stopping

1.26 a. trips
b. trip
c. tripped
d. tripping

1.27 a. washes
b. wash
c. washed
d. washing

1.28 a. watches
b. watch
c. watched
d. watching

1.29 a. works
b. work
c. worked
d. working

1.30 the r is doubled

1.31 the third person singular add -s or -es.

1.32 lain

1.33 chosen

1.34 broken

1.35 ridden

1.36 threw

1.37 flown

1.38 knew

1.39 rung

1.40 grown

1.41 spoken

1.42 driven

1.43 begun

1.44 written

1.45 drank

1.46 blew

1.47 sunk

1.48 frozen

1.49 swam

1.50 sprung

1.51 torn

1.52 Examples:
a. We always begin eating at six o'clock.
b. They usually choose well.
c. You two boys drink a lot or water.

1.53 Examples:
Can you go?
It will shrink if you wash it.
The bell might ring soon.
Could you see the stage?

1.54 Example:
I know how to tread water.

1.55 Example:
To wear that shirt, you need to grow some.

1.56 Example:
You didn't have to break it!

1.57 Example:
He accidentally tore it.

1.58 Example:
His mother forbade him to go.

1.59 Example:
John grew two inches taller last year.

1.60 Example:
The birds might have flown south.

1.61 Example:
It could have been bitten off.

1.62 Example:
That tree surely will have blown down.

1.63 Example:
You should have seen her jump!

1.64 not; nothing; not; no; won't; never

1.65 C.
1.66 C.
1.67 D.N.
1.68 D.N.
1.69 D.N.

SECTION TWO

2.1 a. tenderer
b. tenderest
2.2 a. littler or less
b. littlest or least
2.3 a. abler
b. ablest
2.4 a. idler
b. idlest
2.5 a. holier
b. holiest
2.6 a. narrower
b. narrowest
2.7 a. handsomer
b. handsomest
2.8 a. livelier
b. liveliest
2.9 a. remoter
b. remotest
2.10 a. pleasanter
b. pleasantest
2.11 a. crueler
b. cruelest
2.12 a. quieter
b. quietest
2.13 a. better
b. best
2.14 a. more gentlemanly
b. most gentlemanly
2.15 a. more blessed
b. most blessed
2.16 a. more powerful
b. most powerful
2.17 a. handsomer
b. handsomest
2.18 a. abler
b. ablest
2.19 a. more sacred
b. most sacred
2.20 a. drier
b. driest
2.21 a. larger
b. largest
2.22 a. bigger
b. biggest
2.23 a. fitter
b. fittest
2.24 a. more content
b. most content
2.25 <u>Better</u>
a. dry morsel eaten in quietness
b. many sacrifices eaten with strife
or
a. dry morsel with many sacrifices
b. quietness with strife
2.26 <u>how much more</u>
the hearts of the children of men
with Hell and destruction
2.27 <u>more acceptable</u>
doing justice and judgment with
sacrifice
2.28 <u>Better</u>
a. little with the fear of the Lord
b. great treasure and trouble
therewith.
2.29 <u>Better</u>
a. dinner of herbs where love is
b. stalled ox where hatred is
or
a. dinner of herbs with a stalled ox
b. love with hatred
2.30 a. most high
b. mightiest
2.31 a. most unrighteous
b. most wicked
2.32 a. best
b. most best (D.C.)
2.33 a. more handsome
b. more ugly

2.34 speedier
2.35 unworthiest
2.36 a. more exceeding (twice)
b. more just
2.37 Examples:
a. The sons of Zion are compared with fine gold, to show their worthiness, and with earthen pitchers, to show lack of proper esteem.
b. A lion and a bear are compared with a wicked ruler — all have fierceness that can destroy.
c. A person who curses his parents is compared with a lamp's being put out. The darkness of his life or his soul will be permanent and unchangeable.
d. A mother bear robbed of her cubs is regarded as less dangerous than the destruction caused by the actions of a fool.
e. Having the humble spirit of a poor person is better than dividing riches obtained at someone else's expense.
2.38 teacher check
2.39 singing; dancing; squealing; capering; whinnying; snorting; contorting; prancing; dancing
2.40 Any order:
a. subject
b. object
c. predicate nominative or object of a preposition
2.41 Either order:
a. a complement
b. an object
2.42 Example:
Falling slowly, the snowflakes filled the air.
2.43 Example:
The boy sliding into third is my brother.
2.44 Example:
Playing the piano takes skill.
2.45 Example:
He taught swimming last summer.
2.46 Example:
He is skilled in drawing.

SECTION THREE

3.1 hearing (sound)
3.2 through onomatopoeia and the content emphasis
3.3 Example:
Poetry, has three characteristics: content, effect, and form. It is pleasant, having patterns of sound, and often rhyme. It deals with truth, beauty, or love, etc.
3.4 classification or type
3.5 Examples:
big; country; open; ready; dried; harvest time; slowdrawn; clear; brown; gray; green; intertwined; sagging
3.6 The country is ready for harvest time.
3.7 Examples:
a. idealized picture of life in the country
b. enjoyment of visual images
c. includes rhythm; rhyme; inverted expressions; unified, compact composition; and poetic language.
3.8 teacher check
3.9 Either order:
a. tragedy
b. comedy
3.10 dramatic conventions
3.11 Shakespeare
3.12 a story that is told to explain or to teach something
3.13 a speech made by an actor to himself

3.14 a story with a well defined plot easily told through dialogue and through the actions of characters who are portrayed by actors

3.15 helper check

3.16 the Italian word *novella* meaning story; popular in the medieval period

3.17 Richardson's Pamela

3.18
a. problem/conflict
b. complications
c. climax
d. dénouement

3.19 teacher check

3.20 Any order:
a. carefully created
b. compact
c. unified

3.21 teacher check

SECTION ONE

1.1 Examples:
enterprise, retinue, bankrupt, beset, alien

1.2 teacher check

1.3 teacher check

1.4 Money does not buy happiness or security.

1.5 b

1.6 Examples:
cubits, categorized, covenant, substance

1.7 teacher check

1.8 Hebrews 11:1 says "... faith is the substance of things hoped for, the evidence of things not seen."

1.9 d

1.10 chronological order or time sequence

1.11 He wants us to follow Noah's example and believe God when we cannot see the way for ourselves.

1.12 a. first
b. then
c. when
d. after

1.13 Examples:
ominously, sideboard, sentinels

1.14 teacher check

1.15 The old room was familiar, but something seemed out of place.

1.16 d

1.17 The author emphasized the gloomy light. He used words that foreshadowed trouble: "As long as Aunt Susan was alive," "ominously," and "cautiously."

1.18 c

1.19 opposite the hallway door, on the right wall, to the right, or to the left.

1.20 Examples:
technology, inflation, hydrocarbons, contaminate, depleted, endeavor

1.21 teacher check

1.22 The development of solar technology is vital to the American way of life.

1.23 b

1.24 Solar technology will make the United States energy independent.

1.25 teacher check

1.26 Any order:
a. to tell a story
b. to inform
c. to analyze
d. to persuade
e. to criticize
f. to convince
or to teach, to relate an incident, to give directions

1.27 true

1.28 true

1.29 false

1.30 false

1.31 true

1.32 a. I recognize the words.
b. I attach meaning to the words.
c. I fuse the meanings into an idea.
d. I dig out the implied meanings.
e. I react to what I read.

1.33 chronological order

1.34 topic sentence

1.35 spatial order

1.36 Either order:
a. ascending
b. descending

1.37 The topic sentence may not reveal the purpose when the author intends to convince or persuade the reader to change beliefs, attitudes, and so forth.
1.38 Examples:
parcel, pollutants, detrimental
1.39 teacher check
1.40 teacher check
1.41 A chemical dump in upstate New York has turned into a threat to children and mothers-to-be in that community.
1.42 d
1.43 fourteen
1.44 Examples; any order:
a. tax write off
b. play ground
c. deformed child
d. tragedy
1.45 Example:
They detract from the purpose because they focus our attention on the horror of the situation, away from the causes of and solutions to the problem.
1.46 teacher check
1.47 student check
1.48 Examples:
secular, theology
1.49 teacher check
1.50 teacher check
1.51 Christian youths who decide to live their business lives as well as their personal lives for the Lord, decide to go to Christian colleges instead of secular universities.
1.52 c
1.53 false
1.54 true
1.55 false
1.56 true
1.57 true
1.58 false
1.59 teacher check
1.60 Examples:
proponents, environment, sabotage, operative
1.61 teacher check
1.62 Proponents of nuclear power plants have not considered the hazards involved in operative atomic power plants.
1.63 a
1.64 no
1.65 no
1.66 no
1.67 yes
1.68 yes
1.69 no
1.70 Examples:
a. Any news magazine: Time, Newsweek, U.S. News and World Report
b. Up to date encyclopedia: *World Book, Britannica....*
c. Scientific journals, encyclopedias
d. Newsletter from power companies and environmentalist groups in students area. Include names depending on locality.
1.71 Examples:
accrued, seniority, previous, incumbent
1.72 teacher check
1.73 *The Middletown Daily News* endorses Representative Jay Miller in the race for congressman, against new-comer, Irene Smith.
1.74 d
1.75 He is in line for important committee assignments and has provided outstanding leadership.
1.76 She is a new-comer, apparently without prominent supporters.

1.77 teacher check

1.78 Example:
reluctant, surrogate, adversary, erroneous, symbolic

1.79 teacher check

1.80 The county legislature should not fund the local day care center because day care leads to the destruction of the American family.

1.81 a

1.82 A woman's place is in the home.

1.83 none

1.84 Example:
"A woman's place is in the home" will be chosen by some students.
"There is no need for county-sponsored day care."

1.85 She could be widowed, separated, or divorced. Her husband may be ill or disabled. Her husband may be unable to find work. She may be single and need day care for a niece, nephew, or an adopted child. She may be an unwed mother.

SECTION TWO

2.1 three

2.2 nonfiction

2.3 nonfiction

2.4 fiction

2.5-2.7 Any order:

2.5 fiction

2.6 poetry

2.7 nonfiction

2.8 teacher check

2.9 counseling

2.10 about 120

2.11 financial aid

2.12 July

2.13 240

2.14 clothing

2.15 November

2.16 The need is greater in a cold month that includes a holiday season.

2.17 teacher check

2.18 80°

2.19 August 5

2.20 August 3

2.21 seven

2.22 80°

2.23 teacher check

2.24 six

2.25 Rich

2.26 Elks County

2.27 200

2.28 100 families

2.29 Summer Youth Employment Program

2.30 They returned to school.

2.31 9%

2.32 26%

2.33 Any order:
a. bar graph
b. line graph
c. pictograph
d. pie graph

2.34 line graphs

2.35 pictograph

2.36 pie graph

2.37 teacher check

2.38 Flight 601

2.39 Flight 225

2.40 Gate 18
2.41 10:55
2.42 Rochester
2.43 teacher check
2.44 teacher check
2.45 c
2.46 h
2.47 e
2.48 a
2.49 b
2.50 g
2.51 d
2.52 i
2.53 true
2.54 true
2.55 false
2.56 false
2.57 true
2.58 true
2.59 false

SECTION THREE

3.1 a. lazy - hazy
b. should - would
c. silly - lily
d. ought - thought
3.2 eight
3.3 two
3.4 four
3.5 Any order
a. oughtn't to should
b. couldn't to toil
c. shouldn't to ought
3.6 Example:
They create a comic effect, making the reader laugh.
3.7 It is frail not able to hold anything.
3.8 teacher check
3.9 A
A
B
C
B
D
D
C
E
E
3.10 teacher check
3.11 teacher check
3.12 teacher check
3.13 a. compassionate; two iambic feet
b. football player; two trochaic feet
c. pin curls; one trochaic foot
d. mahogany; two iambic feet
e. electric clock; two iambic feet
3.14 Examples:
a. renew
b. police
c. sincere
d. submit
e. again
f. going
g. answer
h. runway
i. charter
j. Bible
3.15 teacher check
3.16 teacher check

3.17
a. tape recorder; two trochaic feet
b. overpaid laborer; two dactylic feet
c. music theory; two trochaic feet
d. by the light of the silvery moon; three anapestic feet
e. three ring circus; two trochaic feet
f. mystical happening; two dactylic feet
g. Thanksgiving Day; two iambic feet.
h. Wednesday night prayer meeting; two dactylic feet
i. Genesis; one dactylic foot
j. I came, I saw, I conquered Gaul; four iambic feet

3.18
a. trochaic
b. tum-ta
c. Example: writing

3.19
a. anapestic
b. ta-ta-tum
c. Example: disappoint

3.20
a. dactylic
b. tum-ta-ta
c. Example: strawberry

3.21 i
3.22 g
3.23 l
3.24 a
3.25 j
3.26 b
3.27 d
3.28 e
3.29 n
3.30 k
3.31 c
3.32 f
3.33 teacher check

3.34 Any order:
a. trimeter
b. tetrameter
c. pentameter

3.35 Examples:
a. little
b. frozen
c. darkest
d. evening
e. harness
f. lovely

3.36
He clasps the crag with crooked hands A
Close to the sun in lonely lands, A
Ringed with the azure world, he stands. A
The wrinkled sea beneath him crawls; B
He watches from his mountain walls, B
And like a thunderbolt he falls. B

3.37 teacher check

3.38
"O pardon me thou bleeding piece of earth,
That I am meek and gentle with these butchers!
Thou art the ruins of the noblest man
That ever lived in the tide of times.
Woe to the hand that shed this costly blood!"

3.39 teacher check
3.40 blank verse
3.41 Blank verse is written in regular iambic pentameter. Free verse has no regular rhythm and no rhyme scheme.
3.42 teacher check
3.43 teacher check

3.44 teacher check
3.45 true
3.46 true
3.47 true
3.48 true
3.49 false
3.50 teacher check
3.51 teacher check
3.52 true
3.53 true
3.54 false
3.55 true
3.56 true
3.57 e
3.58 d
3.59 a
3.60 f
3.61 c
3.62 b

SECTION ONE

1.1 true
1.2 false
1.3 true
1.4 true
1.5 false
1.6 Either order:
  a. fear
  b. carelessness
1.7 Example:
  Fear can help a speaker by forcing him to prepare carefully. It can hurt when the speaker thinks about his fears instead of his speech.
1.8 Any order:
  a. sincerity
  b. friendliness
  c. authority
1.9 If a speaker projects sincerity, the audience will relax and listen. Sincerity involves honesty, assurance, naturalness, and enthusiasm.
1.10 error or inacurracy
1.11 through the eyes, the voice, and the body of the speaker
1.12 Either order:
  a. conviction
  b. intelligence
1.13 a speaking too softly
  b. not looking at the audience
  c. wandering from the subject
  d. being disorganized
  e. using conjectures or opinions not supported by facts or specifics
  f. trite expressions
1.14 a. a
  b. c
1.15 b
1.16 a. b
  b. d
  c. e
1.17 a. a
  b. c
  c. d
  d. e
1.18 a. a
  b. b
  c. d
  d. e
1.19 a. a
  b. c
1.20 false
1.21 false
1.22 true
1.23 true
1.24 false
1.25 true
1.26 false
1.27 false
1.28 when to use it
1.29 Any order:
  a. to summarize what has been said
  b. to intensify interest
  c. to create an appropriate closing mood
1.30 point-by-point
1.31 in different words
1.32 an example
1.33 Either order:
  a. your topic
  b. your audience
1.34 Any order:
  a. an irrelevant conclusion
  b. an apologetic conclusion
  c. an inconclusive conclusion
  d. a trite conclusion
1.35 teacher check

1.36 Hint:
Joe was quite effective. His voice strength added impressiveness to the message. He paused appropriately for meaning.
1.37 the accurate production of tone
1.38 variety in voicetone; the range of expressiveness of the voice.
1.39 the power or volume of voice
1.40 Proper breathing produces the energy; the vocal cords act as vibrators to produce the initial sound that is then amplified by the resonaters (throat, mouth, and nasal passages).
1.41 A speaker must breathe regularly, deeply, easily, and often, never letting his speech be breathless or quavery.
1.42 true
1.43 false
1.44 true
1.45 true
1.46 teacher check

SECTION TWO

2.1 false
2.2 true
2.3 false
2.4 false
2.5 true
2.6 true
2.7 true
2.8 true
2.9 true
2.10 listening
2.11 Either order:
a. listening
b. reading
2.12 the larger the vocabulary the more one understands
2.13 experience in hearing different kinds of voices, languages, and patterns of speech
2.14 3
1
5
2
4
6
2.15 Any order:
a. previous knowledge
b. nature of material
c. physiology of listening
d. attention or concentration
e. comprehension
2.16 g
2.17 e
2.18 f
2.19 a
2.20 d
2.21 b
2.22 teacher check
2.23 Any order:
a. Using voice inflections rather than a monotone can make it more meaningful.
b. Pausing used as punctuation can clarify meaning.
c. Unfamiliar vocabulary causes audience attention to lag.
d. Unfamiliar sentence patterns can confuse the listeners.
e. Too long a speech without a break will tire the listener.
2.24 Either order:
a. Important points will usually be marked by the speaker's actions. He may move from the lectern, gesture, or move around more actively.
b. Frequently repeated ideas are usually key ideas.
2.25 teacher check

2.26 Either order:
a. good listening
b. skillful speaking

2.27 Either order:
a. facial expression
b. body movement

2.28 Any order:
a. interested
b. friendly
c. not critical
d. cheerful
e. relaxed but enthusiastic
f. flexible
or tactful
courteous

SECTION THREE

3.1 Any order:
a. griefs
b. joys
c. fears
d. hopes
e. suspicions

3.2 a. redoubles
b. cuts griefs in half (two)

3.3 Any order:
a. toss his thoughts more easily
b. marshall them more orderly
c. see how they look when turned into words
d. make him wax wiser than himself

3.4 a. friends
b. flatterer

3.5 personality

3.6 Any order:
a. use contractions
b. use slang terms
c. use colloquial expressions
d. call your friend by name in the body of the letter
e. underline words for emphasis
f. use expressive punctuation

3.7 informal, or "friendly" letter

3.8 colloquial conversational

3.9 acceptable

3.10 signing it

3.11 an apology

3.12 answer any questions your friend asked

3.13 simply say good-bye without feeling explanation is necessary

3.14 teacher check

3.15 Example:
Write it to the friend and then rewrite it addressing the mother.

3.16 Example:
sincere appreciation for a kindness

3.17 Example:
Dear Mr. and Mrs. Standish,
How can we thank you adequately for the kind hospitality we felt in your home? It is wonderful to meet the people we will know all through eternity. How gracious our Lord is to have sent us your way. Thank you!
Sincerely,
Joan and Debbie

3.18 Example:
Because you have inconvenienced her.

3.19 regret at having caused the inconvenience, appreciation of past kindness

3.20 Example:
It indicates Christian-orientation rather than egocentricity.

3.21 Example:
You can express sympathy, love, and Christian compassion.

3.22 Example:
Don't give him the promises of God, that are not his outside of Christ.

3.23 true

3.24 false

3.25 true

3.26 false

3.27 true

3.28 true

3.29 Any order:
It conveys an important message, it serves as a record of a transaction, and it builds good will.

3.30 Any order:
the heading, the inside address, the salutation, the body, the closing, and the signature

3.31 teacher check

SECTION ONE

1.1 a. an alphabetical arrangement of cards listing books in a library
b. a card in the card catalog listed by the author's name
c. a card in the card catalog listed under the topic or subject of the book
d. a card in the card catalog listed under the title of the book

1.2 Any order:
a. author's name and birthdate
b. title and publication information
c. call numbers
d. description of book
e. additional entries in card catalog

1.3 a. teacher check
b. teacher check
c. teacher check
d. teacher check
e. teacher check

1.4 a. B
b. K
c. R

1.5 c

1.6 l

1.7 h

1.8 a

1.9 j

1.10 i

1.11 k

1.12 e

1.13 b

1.14 k

1.15 Example:
Dewey Decimal

1.16 Example:
yes, at the local college library

1.17 Any order:
a. dictionaries
b. encyclopedias
c. indexes
d. directories
e. handbooks
f. atlases
g. guides
h. yearbooks

1.18 Examples:
a. *World Book Encyclopedia*
b. *Compton's Pictured Encyclopedia*
c. *Encyclopedia Americana*

1.19 Example:
a. drama
b. history of drama
c. kinds of drama (characteristics of)

1.20 Example:
a. similar
b. seems a little simpler

1.21 Example:
a. different
b. more detail

1.22 Example:
 a. the third
 b. more detail
1.23 Examples:
 a. *The World Almanac* is helpful for providing current statistics and facts.
 b. *National Geographic Atlas of the World* contains information about countries and capitals.
 c. not available
 d. *Who's Who in America* provides brief biographical information about important living Americans.
1.24 teacher check
1.25 a. also apprize
 b. also catty-cornered
 c. also catsup, ketchup
 d. choosy
 e. doughnut
 f. Eskimo
 g. see good-by
 h. also juijitsu, juijutsu, jujutsu
 i. also tee shirt (because of the shape)
1.26 after Michel Begon (1638-1710) after Captain Charles Boycott (1832-1897) He was a land agent in Ireland who was "boycotted" by angry tenants. (see chauvin) After Nicholas Chauvin, a French soldier who supported and admired Napoleon. after Anders Dahl (1751-1789) He was a Swedish botanist. from Dunsman or duncemen who were followers of John Duns Scotus, a thirteenth-century theologian resembling Don Quixote, a character in a book by Miguel de Cervantes
1.27 a. to refer to indirectly
 b. to escape or avoid
 c. a group or coalition
 d. a solid, flat-sided piece of wood, stone, metal, ice
 e. light or fair of hair and skin; noun form refers to males
 f. noun form refers to females
 g. (n) strong, heavy, coarse material, usually cotton or flax
 h. (v) to inspect carefully
 i. (n) a group of people assembled to consider issues
 j. (n) the act of talking; advice given; lawyer (v) to advise
 k. to show off
 l. to scoff at, treat with scorn or contempt
 m. having the quality or form of people
 n. merciful or kind
 o. skillful or clever
 p. sincere, open, natural
 q. to give up a right or a claim; surrender
 r. (v) to move up and down or sway back and forth, as a wave (n) a moving swell of water
1.28 Examples:
 a. a revelation; Apocalypse, the last book of the New Testament, Revelation
 b. universal, of interest to all; Catholic, the Christian church governed by the Pope, Roman Catholic
 c. fellowship, sharing; Communion, sharing the Lord's Supper in a worship service
 d. the appearance of something, especially a diety; Ephiphany, the anniversary of the coming of the Wise Men to Bethlehem, January 6
 e. one who likes another; Friend, a Quaker, Society of Friends, a Christian group
 f. origin, creation; Genesis, the first book of the Old Testament describing creation
 g. a strong feeling, a strong emotion; Passion, the suffering of Jesus on the cross
 h. one who has strict religious and moral beliefs; Puritan, a sixteenth- or seventeenth-century member of the church of England who stood for simplification of worship and stricter rules
1.29 OPTIONAL:
 teacher check

1.30 the *Reader's Guide to Periodical Literature*
1.31 periodicals
1.32 Either order:
  a. author
  b. subject
1.33 alphabetically
1.34 Any order:
  a. *Art Index*
  b. *Biography Index*
  c. *Dramatic Index*
  or *Music Index, Statistical Abstract of the United States*
1.35 Either order:
  a. *Familiar Quotations* by Bartlett and Beck
  b. *The Oxford Dictionary of Quotations*
1.36 Example:
  the *New York Times Index*
1.37 a. teacher check
  b. OPTIONAL:
  teacher check
1.38 Example:
  to call a friend or relative whose number you don't know; to locate the number or address of a doctor or other professional or business person you want to contact
1.39 to find the appropriate word to use in a particular paper or article
1.40 the exact intention to be expressed by the word
1.41 a collection of articles, leaflets, and pamphlets placed in folders and filed alphabetically
1.42 d
1.43 b

SECTION TWO

2.1 a. a story
  b. told in action
  c. by actors impersonating characters in the story
2.2 Greece
2.3 Any order:
  a. mystery
  b. miracle
  c. morality
2.4 genre
2.5 Either order:
  a. William Shakespeare
  b. Ben Jonson
  or Christopher Marlowe
2.6 Any order:
  a. little plot or action
  b. character studies
  c. no script; improvise
  d. audience part of cast
2.7 Examples:
  a. yes
  b. Shakespeare's *Hamlet*
2.8 c
2.9 a
2.10 b
2.11 d
2.12 d
2.13 i
2.14 e
2.15 f
2.16 j
2.17 b
2.18 a
2.19 h

2.20 k
2.21 c
2.22 teacher check
2.23 OPTIONAL:
teacher check
2.24 a. read list of characters (picture each)
b. read description of set (visualize it)
c. visualize details of stage setting
d. read dialogue carefully
e. try to analyze characters
2.25 Hint:
Try to imagine a very large, southern home, about the 1880's. Focus on the nursery at nighttime. Are there candles or oil lamps, perhaps a small fireplace? What does the furniture look like? How are the people dressed? (Mrs. Keller might be wearing a long dress with a hoop skirt.) In Act III, try to focus on the action. Read through the stage directions several times, if necessary, so that you can follow the action in your mind.
2.26 OPTIONAL:
Hint:
Look under "Set Design" in the card catalog. If you cannot find an entry in your library, you may find it helpful to look under "Theater," either in the card catalog or in an index to subject headings for the Library of Congress; consult your librarian if you have difficulty. You should be able to find either complete books on the subject, or else chapters within more general books on the theater, again depending upon your library.

SECTION THREE

3.1 Check the encyclopedia and card catalog, then the *Reader's Guide.* You may also find the *New York Times Index* (leading you to other newspapers, if necessary), the vertical file, and bibliographies from books on the topic.
3.2 OPTIONAL
Hint:
Generally requirements include a bachelor's degree from an accredited university; state requirements will differ.
3.3 Either order:
a. blindness
b. being deaf
3.4 a. Anne Sullivan
b. Horace Mann School for the Deaf
3.5 Radcliffe
3.6 *The Story of My Life*
3.7 In the Dewey Decimal system an individual biography is listed under "B."
3.8 The two most logical places are "A" for general works and "P" for language and literature.
3.9-3.11 OPTIONAL:
3.9 teacher check
3.10 teacher check
3.11 teacher check
3.12 Some of the clues suggesting the play's setting include the opening stage directions (dress, 1880's, the doctor's housecall), the doctor's

buggy, the lamp Captain Keller carries, Alexander Graham Bell, the reference to a state poorhouse, $25 a month salary, the railroad as main transportation, the Keller's carriage, Annie's clothes that Helen "tries" on, the pitcher and basin for water on the chest, and the water pump.

3.13 OPTIONAL:
teacher check

3.14 a. Bartlett's *Familiar Quotations* gives the full proverb as "Tall oaks from little acorns grow," noting that these were lines written for a school declamation for Ephraim Farrar, aged 7, of New Ipswich, New Hampshire, in 1791. Actually the line completes a couplet:
"Large streams from little fountains flow.
Tall oaks from little acorns grow."
(Bartlett, John. *Familiar Quotations*. 13th ed. Boston: Little, Brown, and Co., 1955, p. 401a.)

b. The quotation applies to the play because it means that insignificant events may lead eventually to her associating words with actual things and people.

3.15 Example:
a. yes, mama
b. Perhaps one reason "mama" and "dada" may be among the first words a baby learns is that he or she is absolutely dependent upon parents at this age. Perhaps many parents ask their children to repeat these words to them, also.
c. An infant may communicate in various ways including eye contact, smiles, sounds (unhappy ones like crying as well as happy ones like cooing), and touch.

3.16 One similarity between Helen's story and the life of a practicing Christian is the need for discipline; we must learn and practice obedience to God. Another similarity is the metaphor of sight and blindness; without knowledge of God, we are spiritually "blind."

3.17 teacher check

3.18 teacher check

3.19 OPTIONAL:
teacher check

SECTION ONE

1.1 d
1.2 a
1.3 false
1.4 false
1.5 true
1.6 true
1.7 true
1.8 true
1.9 true
1.10 false
1.11 true
1.12 b
1.13 a
1.14 c
1.15 d
1.16 c
1.17 Example:
author or teller of the story; one that the reader is aware of
1.18 false
1.19 true
1.20 true
1.21 true
1.22 true
1.23 a
1.24 a
1.25 c
1.26 b
1.27 a
1.28 yes
1.29 yes
1.30 yes
1.31 yes
1.32 no
1.33 e
1.34 a
1.35 f
1.36 c
1.37 b
1.38 Any order:
a. emphasis on character
b. representation of characters with extreme care
c. character is clearly developed
d. incident or episode is secondary
1.39 Any order:
a. individual episodes
b. incidents generally unrelated
c. loose plot structure
d. chronological order
e. excitement generated by series of unrelated incidents
1.40 Daniel Defoe
1.41 d
1.42 d
1.43 b
1.44 c
1.45 true
1.46 false
1.47 true

1.48 false
1.49 true
1.50 false
1.51 c
1.52 e
1.53 a
1.54 f
1.55 b
1.56 a poem that treats of shepherds and their life in the country
1.57 praise by a shepherd for a loved one in a poem
1.58 a singing match between two shepherds
1.59 poem for a dead friend
1.60 Example subjects:
1. poetry about the country
2. friends portrayed as shepherds
3. artistic creations of the countryside
4. poem about rural people
5. a method for writing complex things simply

1.61 d
1.62 a
1.63 f
1.64 g
1.65 h
1.66 c
1.67 b
1.68 i
1.69-1.74 Examples:
1.69 day-by-day record of events, often personal and private
1.70 account of daily events, not as personal as a diary
1.71 life and times of a central character
1.72 a prose work, frank, witty, gossipy estimate of contemporary
1.73 a short narration of an event of interest; no plot or unity
1.74 a collection of miscellaneous sayings, bits of information about an individual
1.75 knights, kings, ladies in distress, heroism, religious faith
1.76 mystery, fantasy
1.77 stories of Germanic and English tradition
1.78 stories of Charlemagne, William of Orange
1.79 legends of Alexander the Great, city of Thebes, city of Troy
1.80 stories about King Arthur
1.81 a
1.82 b
1.83 c
1.84 a
1.85 d
1.86 d
1.87 k
1.88 b
1.89 e
1.90 i
1.91 c
1.92 j

1.93 h
1.94 a
1.95 f
1.96 d

1.97 use of letters
1.98 many points of view; to make remarks about events and characters; reader is right there
1.99 introduced the exploration of inner self of characters
1.100 f
1.101 d
1.102 f
1.103 b
1.104 c
1.105 f
1.106 a
1.107 e
1.108 true
1.109 false
1.110 false
1.111 false
1.112 true
1.113 magic, mystery, chivalry, ghosts, strange houses, horror
1.114 single social class, manners, customs, habits, conventions, accuracy, detail
1.115 reconstructs past out of scholarship
1.116 works out a central problem through characters or incidents
1.117 involves a crime, solved logically from clues by a detective
1.118 interior characterization, deals with motives, circumstances, internal action
1.119 faithful to the speech, habits, manners, history, and so on, of a geographical region
1.120 deals with a problem, but with rigid solution
1.121 true
1.122 false
1.123 true
1.124 true
1.125 true
1.126 c
1.127 a
1.128 d
1.129 c
1.130 a
1.131 true
1.132 false
1.133 false
1.134 false
1.135 true
1.136 a, b, c, d, f, g, i, j, k, l
1.137 true
1.138 true
1.139 false
1.140 false
1.141 true

1.142 a. expressionism
b. expressionism
c. impressionism
d. impressionism
e. impressionism
f. expressionism
g. expressionism
h. impressionism
i. expressionism

1.143 literature

1.144 never

1.145 many

1.146 another's

1.147 middle-class

1.148 b

1.149 c

1.150 a

1.151 d

1.152 c

SECTION TWO

2.1 Any order:
a. *Five Weeks in a Balloon*
b. *Journey to the Center of the Earth*
c. *The Adventures of Captain Hatteras*
d. *Twenty Thousand Leagues Under the Sea*
e. *Around the World in Eighty Days*

2.2 Any order:
a. a work of fantasy
b. breaks away from reality
c. takes place in unreal world
d. based on science fact or assumption

2.3 Example:
This novel has the four components listed in 2.2.

2.4-2.7 Examples:

2.4 scientist, an authority, liked his scholarly reputation, zoologist, botanist, geologist, mineralogist

2.5 Belgian, brave, devoted, impassive, self-taught, exceptional in natural history classification, narrow specialty his life, ten years employed with Aronnax, strong constitution, physically strong, thirty years old, very formal

2.6 Canadian, forty years old, six feet tall, powerful build, piercing eyes, extraordinary as a harpooner, cool, courageous, cunning, uncommunicative, sometimes violent, hot-headed, brave

2.7 good sailor, soul of his ship, believed it was a whale and he was after it, determined

2.8 narwhal but ten times larger than anything known

2.9 Any order:
a. a floating island or reef
b. a monster of colossal size
c. a submarine with powerful engines

2.10 a. Psalm 74:14 — many headed
b. Isaiah 27:1 — sea dragon, piercing serpent, crooked serpent
c. Job 41:1 — too big to fish for
d. Psalm 104:26 — a very big sea animal

2.11 false

2.12 true

2.13 false

2.14 false
2.15 true
2.16 Hint:
Many things can be written and can be organized in various ways, but the questions above should guide you.
2.17 Example:
He loves its size and immensity, its life; it's a reservoir, and a place to be independent.
2.18 point of view
2.19 first-person
2.20 limited
2.21 omniscient
2.22 self-effacing
2.23 Pierre Aronnax
2.24 first person
2.25 first and third
2.26 Hint:
Answer should include that he does not like society, he loves the sea, he's a scientist, strict, and a leader.
2.27 episodes
2.28 logical
2.29 incident
2.30 causes
2.31 Example:
Ned Land wanting off the ship; Nemo wants Land's word and the others not to escape or harm anything; the ideas of the passengers about the sea and what they see; Captain Nemo and society; conflict between rumor and truth; and many more conflicts
2.32 false
2.33 true
2.34 true
2.35 false
2.36 true
2.37 Hint:
A good place is Aronnax's thoughts in Chapter XXV. The student should give reasons for his answer.
2.38 d
2.39 c
2.40 a
2.41 b
2.42 a
2.43 Hint:
Discuss Captain Nemo's physical attributes, outlook on life, education, manners, and so on. Then compare Captain Nemo and the other character you choose.
2.44 false
2.45 false
2.46 false
2.47 true
2.48 true
2.49 Nemo — objective and scientific to revengeful
Aronnax — sure to somewhat doubtful of all he knew
2.50 His attitudes and approach to things remained the same.
2.51 teacher check
2.52 teacher check

SECTION THREE

3.1 teacher check
3.2 teacher check
3.3 a. the art or principles of making careful judgment
b. act or process of bringing out the meaning
3.4 The author-narrator builds all three by giving reports of the "monster" from reliable sources and recounts incidents of the monster's attacks. The introduction of the narrator, Aronnax, in Chapter II further adds to the interest because he is a scientist who believes that the monster may be real, may be a giant narwhal.
3.5 Hints:
excitement, discovery, curiosity, exhilaration, discovery pushes them over physical hardship
3.6 a. everything to show man nature and God
b. mistrusts it, practical
c. a classifier, no imagination
d. science for power and revenge
3.7 Aronnax an astute observer; Nemo an avid collector

3.8-3.12 Examples:
3.8 No, because he wants the world his way and considers no one else.
3.9 Science is good in its place.
3.10 Everything begins with God as creator.
3.11 Yes, he is emotional and he wants his way.
No, he will stop and help his fellow man.
3.12 Yes, Conseil's loyalty is an example of a "Christian" attitude.
3.13 What does the writer say
3.14 How does he say it
3.15 Was what he said worthwhile
3.16 methods
3.17 fictional
3.18 teacher check
3.19 teacher check
3.20 teacher check
3.21 false
3.22 true
3.23 true
3.24 false
3.25 false
3.26 teacher check

SECTION ONE

1.1 true
1.2 true
1.3 false
1.4 true
1.5 true
1.6 false
1.7 false
1.8 true
1.9 true
1.10 true
1.11 g
1.12 a
1.13 c
1.14 f
1.15 d
1.16 Any order:
  a. written
  b. spoken
  c. nonverbal
1.17 Any order:
  a. a pattern of sounds
  b. a collection of words
  c. a system of word arrangement
  d. elements of grammar
1.18 the Secretary of State
1.19 Bill's house
1.20 Iowa
1.21
1.22 Chevrolet
1.23 Easter
1.24 Uncle Bill
1.25
1.26 the Supreme Court
1.27 The Chicago Tribune
1.28 Greek gods
1.29 the Bible
1.30
1.31 abstract
1.32 collective
1.33 concrete
1.34 rodeos
1.35 horses
1.36 automobiles
1.37 leaves
1.38 hearts
1.39 stories
1.40 lunches
1.41 tomatoes
1.42 globes
1.43 dictionaries
1.44 spaces
1.45 wishes
1.46 mottoes
1.47 shoes
1.48 shelves
1.49 Mary's
1.50 Jones'
1.51 the farmer's
1.52 the mother-in-law's
1.53 boys'
1.54 banker's
1.55 coach's
1.56 team's
1.57 businessmen's
1.58 appositive
1.59 predicate
1.60 a. more beautiful
  b. most beautiful
1.61 a. angrier
  b. angriest
1.62 a. bluer
  b. bluest
1.63 a. more sensible
  b. most sensible
1.64 a. more correct
  b. most correct
1.65 I have had
1.66 they had

1.67 you had had
1.68 he, she, it has
1.69 you will have had
1.70 he, she, it will have
1.71 passive
1.72 active
1.73 passive
1.74 active
1.75 passive
1.76 intransitive
1.77 transitive
1.78 intransitive
1.79 intransitive
1.80 intransitive
1.81 indicative
1.82 imperative
1.83 indicative
1.84 subjunctive
1.85 imperative
1.86 Any order:
 a. verbs
 b. adjectives
 c. other adverbs
1.87 almost anywhere
1.88 badly
1.89 less
1.90 a. a part of speech used in place of a noun
 b. a part of speech that shows a relationship between its object and another word in the sentence
 c. a part of speech that connects or joins words or groups of words
1.91 Any order:
 a. nominative
 b. objective
 c. possessive
1.92 Any order:
 a. masculine
 b. feminine
 c. neuter
1.93 relative
1.94 interrogative
1.95 demonstrative
1.96 Example; any order:
 a. in
 b. above
 c. with
 d. to
 e. between
 f. off
1.97 Examples; any order:
 a. and
 b. but
 c. or
1.98 Example; either order:
 a. both . . . and
 b. neither . . . nor
1.99 Example; any order:
 a. after
 b. because
 c. until
 d. before
1.100 Example; any order:
 a. therefore
 b. consequently
 c. however
 d. nevertheless
1.101 gerund phase
1.102 participial phrase
1.103 infinitive phrase
1.104 appositive phrase
1.105 adjective; <u>who has the ball</u>
1.106 adverb; <u>if the rain stops soon</u>
1.107 noun; <u>Wherever you choose to go</u>
1.108 adjective; <u>that faces the post office</u>

SECTION TWO

2.1 Either order:
a. subject
b. predicate

2.2 Any order:
a. predicate adjective
b. predicate nominative
c. direct object
d. indirect object

2.3 i.o.
2.4 p.a.
2.5 d.o.
2.6 p.n.
2.7 p.a.
2.8 p.n.
2.9 s
2.10 d.o.
2.11 The cat ate the rat.

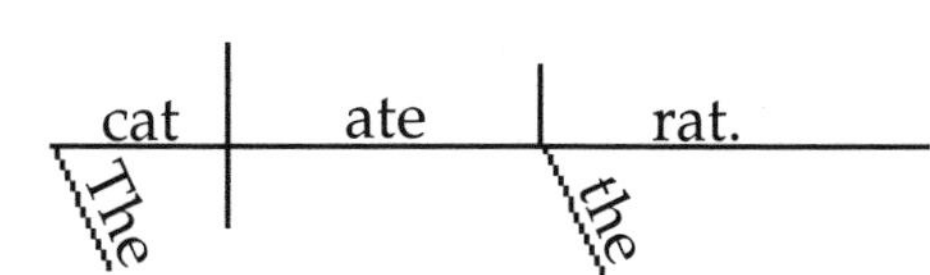

2.12 Reading from the Bible is inspiring.

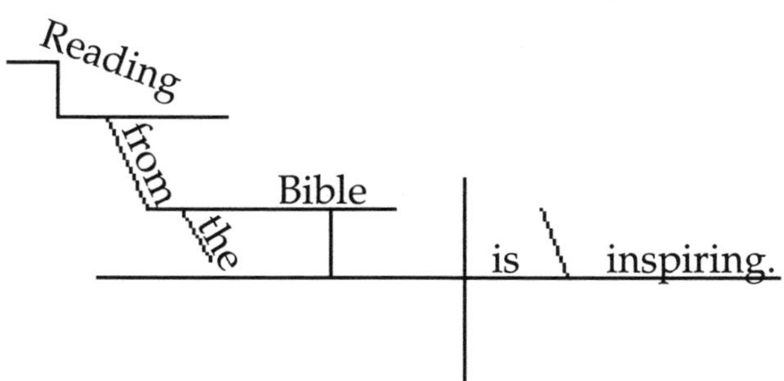

2.13 The man in the grey suit tipped his hat.

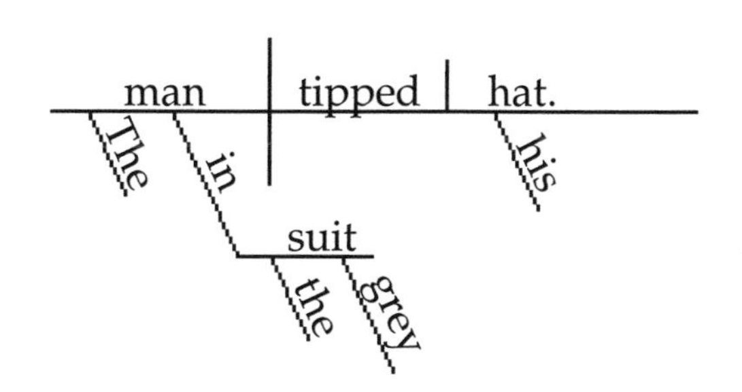

2.14 teacher check

2.15 Although they looked delicious Billy's cookies were made with baking soda instead of sugar.
2.16 Joe and Gary bowl on the same team, and their team is in first place.
2.17 Example:
Because he skidded to the left, Tom narrowly avoided hitting his baby brother's toys.
2.18 teacher check
2.19 Any order:
a. letter of thanks
b. note of apology
c. letter of congratulations
d. letter of condolence

2.20 false
2.21 true
2.22 false
2.23 false
2.24 false
2.25 true
2.26 a. heading
b. inside address
c. salutation
d. body
e. closing
f. signature

2.27 false
2.28 true
2.29 true
2.30 false
2.31 true
2.32 b
2.33 a
2.34 c
2.35 b
2.36 d
2.37 false
2.38 true
2.39 true
2.40 false
2.41 true

SECTION THREE

3.1 P
3.2 Q
3.3 A
3.4 R
3.5 E-F
3.6 T
3.7 A
3.8 S
3.9 M
3.10 L
3.11 Any order:
a. author's name and date of birth
b. title of the book, place of publication, and date
c. call number
d. number of pages and size of pages
e. additional entries in the card catalog
3.12 an encyclopedia
3.13 an almanac
3.14 Either order:
a. Atlases
b. gazetteers
3.15 yearbooks
3.16 ME "tapistry," modif. of MF "tapisserie," fr "tapisser" to carpet, fr OF "tapis" carpet fr. Gk "tapes" rug or carpet.
3.17 F "sardonique" fr Gk "sardonios" distainfully or humorously skeptical
3.18 L. from Gk "hippopotamos" fr. "hipp" + "potamos" river fr. "peteshai" to fly
3.19 ME fr. L "clement" "clemens"
3.20 Alter of ME "tine"
3.21 Examples:
a. amends
b. expiation
a. significant
b. momentous
a. hue
b. tint
3.22 Optional; teacher check
3.23 Optional; teacher check
3.24 false
3.25 false
3.26 true
3.27 true
3.28 true
3.29 true
3.30 May
3.31 650 kilowatt hours
3.32 July
3.33 200 kilowatt hours
3.34 700 kilowatt hours
3.35 Example:
The rest of the paragraph would probably discuss the fact that oil is no longer available in great supply and that nuclear energy is dangerous. Thus the best alternative America has is to learn to utilize solar energy.
3.36 a. 1
b. 3
c. 2
3.37 a. 2
b. 1
c. 3
3.38 a. 2
b. 5
c. 4
d. 1
e. 3
3.39 c
3.40 b
3.41 a
3.42 d
3.43 c
3.44 e

3.45 d
3.46 a
3.47 c
3.48 g
3.49 b
3.50 b
3.51 c
3.52 a
3.53 b
3.54 b
3.55 d
3.56 false
3.57 false
3.58 true
3.59 false
3.60 false
3.61 true
3.62 true
3.63 true
3.64 false
3.65 true
3.66 b
3.67 j
3.68 i
3.69 c
3.70 h
3.71 g
3.72 f
3.73 a
3.74 e
3.75 d

Notes

SELF TEST 1

1.01 true
1.02 true
1.03 false
1.04 false
1.05 true
1.06 false
1.07 true
1.08 false
1.09 true
1.010 true
1.011 a
1.012 b
1.013 b
1.014 a
1.015 b
1.016 c
1.017 b
1.018 c
1.019 b
1.020 a
1.021 sentence
1.022 proper
1.023 abstract
1.024 collective
1.025 compound
1.026 concrete
1.027 churches
1.028 skies
1.029 hyphen
1.030 comparative
1.031 A compound word may be written as one word; it may be hyphenated; or it may be two words.
1.032 Examples:
To form the plural of compound nouns with more than one word or in hyphenated form, add the appropriate plural sign to the main word.
or
To form the plural of compound nouns written as one word, add the appropriate plural sign to the end.

SELF TEST 2

2.01 b
2.02 h
2.03 k
2.04 a
2.05 i
2.06 j
2.07 d
2.08 g
2.09 e
2.010 c
2.011 regular
2.012 auxiliary
2.013 mood
2.014 time
2.015 subject
2.016 I shall have had
2.017 you will be
2.018 you had been seen

2.019 active
2.020 conjugation
2.021 b
2.022 c
2.023 b
2.024 c
2.025 d
2.026 c
2.027 b
2.028 a
2.029 d
2.030 c
2.031 To form the plural of a noun ending in y preceded by a consonant, change y to i and add -es.
2.032 a. I shall have been seen
b. You will have been seen
c. He/she/it will have been seen
d. We shall have been seen
e. You will have been seen
f. They will have been seen

SELF TEST 3

3.01 true
3.02 true
3.03 true
3.04 false
3.05 true
3.06 false
3.07 false
3.08 true
3.09 false
3.010 true
3.011 c
3.012 b
3.013 c
3.014 b
3.015 c
3.016 a
3.017 b
3.018 b
3.019 a
3.020 a
3.021 he
3.022 objective
3.023 demonstrative
3.024 antecedent
3.025 preposition
3.026 conjunction
3.027 subordinating conjunctions
3.028 conjunctive adverbs
3.029 indefinite
3.030 correlative
3.031 Example:
A prepositional phrase functions in a sentence as a modifier. It modifies the word to which the preposition relates its objects.
3.032 I, you, he, she, it

SELF TEST 4

4.01 c
4.02 j
4.03 e
4.04 h
4.05 a
4.06 k
4.07 b
4.08 i
4.09 d
4.010 g
4.011 predicate
4.012 interrogative
4.013 phrase
4.014 a. gerund

b. noun
4.015 a. participial
b. adjective
4.016 subordinate
4.017 adjective
4.018 adverb
4.019 b
4.020 d
4.021 a
4.022 c
4.023 b
4.024 a
4.025 d
4.026 b
4.027 a
4.028 a
4.029-4.030 Examples:
4.029 Neither can stand by itself; both can be used as adjectives and adverbs.
4.030 A subordinate clause contains a subject and a predicate and is usually introduced by either a subordinate conjunction or a relative pronoun. A prepositional phrase contains neither a subject nor a predicate, only the preposition, its object, and any modifiers of the object.

SELF TEST 5

5.01 false
5.02 true
5.03 true
5.04 false
5.05 true
5.06 f
5.07 c
5.08 a
5.09 b
5.010 e
5.011 conjunction
5.012 subordinating conjunction
5.013 subject
5.014 direct object
5.015 predicate nominative
5.016 indirect object
5.017 predicate adjective
5.018 complement
5.019 predicate
5.020 passive
5.021 i.o.
5.022 p.a.
5.023 p.n.
5.024 s.
5.025 p.
5.026 a
5.027 b
5.028 b
5.029 c
5.030 b

5.031

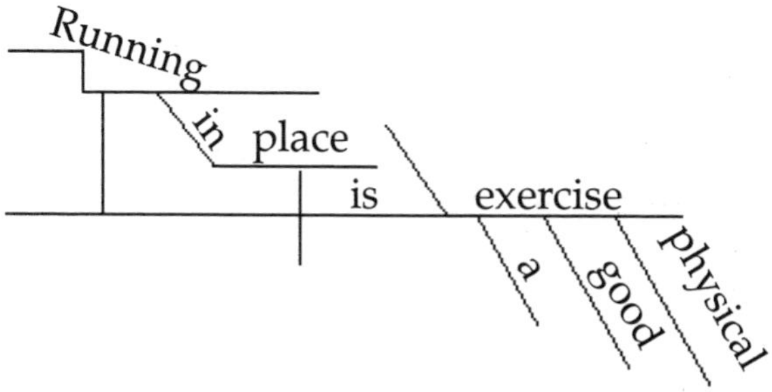

Running
in
place
is
exercise
a
good
physical

5.032

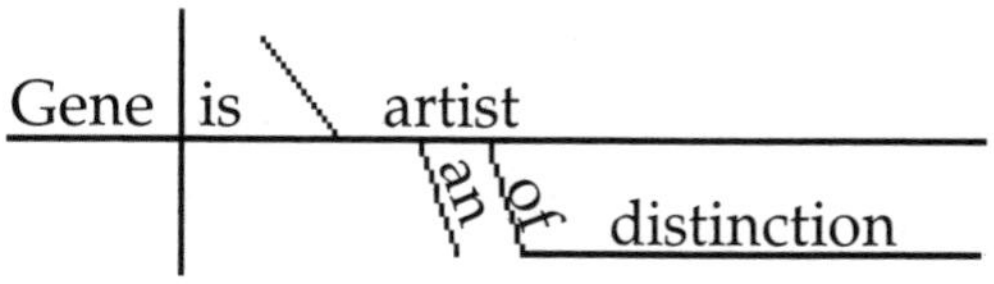

Gene
is
artist
an
of
distinction

SELF TEST 1

1.01 linguistics
1.02 linguists

1.03 Any order:
a. a pattern of sounds
b. a collection of words
c. a system of word arrangement
d. the elements of grammar
1.04 emigrate
1.05 morphology
1.06 words (or language, or tongues)
1.07 Latin
1.08 d
1.09 i
1.010 g
1.011 a
1.012 k
1.013 j
1.014 b
1.015 e
1.016 h
1.017 c
1.018 Hint:
You should have mentioned all four of the things common to all true language. Animals cannot acquire any of these because of physical and mental (their tongues, jaws, lungs, minds) limitations.
1.019 a. You will be able to communicate with more of the world's people.
b. By learning a second language, you can better understand English.
c. Learning a second language helps you to understand people of different cultures.
1.020 The origin of language is as early as man. God is the source of language. Since man was created in God's image, man was created with the capacity to communicate freely with God and other men.
1.021 Hint:
Discuss the well-organized language before Abraham's time. Tell how perfectly Adam used language when he named the living creatures. Point to the fact that God had communicated to Noah complicated plans for building the ark. Noah was a preacher of righteousness.
1.022 Any order:
a. spoken words
b. written words
c. nonverbal expressions
1.023 Any order:
a. Has man always had language?
b. After the confusion of tongues at the Tower of Babel, did the many resulting language families still have anything in common?
c. Does a person need to study any language other than his own?

SELF TEST 2

2.01 c

2.02 i

2.03 h

2.04 a

2.05 j

2.06 d

2.07 g

2.08 e

2.09 f

2.010 b

2.011 b

2.012 a

2.013 c

2.014 b

2.015 c

2.016 b

2.017 a

2.018 b

2.019 b

2.020 a

2.021 Either order:
 a. spoken
 b. nonverbal

2.022 Either order:
 a. Latin
 b. Greek

2.023 order

2.024 Either order:
 a. Angles
 b. Saxons

2.025 Either order:
 a. Latin
 b. Greek

2.026 speech

2.027 When people began to say their vowels with a glide there was a great change in spelling from long vowels to diphthongs.

2.028 Chaucer led the change to Middle English. Chaucer's writings represent examples of the language in transition. Sentences began to fall into a regular pattern of subject-verb-object, and word endings were changed. Word order became more important than word endings.

SELF TEST 3

3.01 aid to memory

3.02 Any order:
a. written
b. spoken
c. nonverbal

3.03 context

3.04 u

3.05 root

3.06 Iraq

3.07 peers

3.08 able II— complete word except for e

3.09 able III — able always after i

3.010 able I — able after complete word

3.011 ible VII — immediate -tion form

3.012 ible VI — incomplete word takes -ible

3.013 able IV — has a form based on the letter a

3.014 able V — able after hard c

3.015 able I — complete word

3.016 2

3.017 7

3.018 1

3.019 3

3.020 5

3.021 4

3.022 6

3.023-3.025 Any order: (Sound patterns also possible answer)

3.023 words

3.024 system of word arrangement

3.025 grammatical structure

3.026-3.030 Answers may vary; examples are given:

3.026 insect (cut)

3.027 autograph (write)

3.028 monologue, theology (talk or knowledge)

3.029 sophomore, sophisticated (wise, wisdom)

3.030 tangible (touch)

3.031 c

3.032 e

3.033 a

3.034 b

3.035 d

SELF TEST 1

1.01 formerly

1.02 admirable
1.03 illusion
1.04 furnish
1.05 farce
1.06 short
1.07 TH
1.08 th
1.09 zh
1.010 ə
1.011 a
1.012 b
1.013 b
1.014 c
1.015 d
1.016 b
1.017 b
1.018 c
1.019 c
1.020 a
1.021 b
1.022 d
1.023 a
1.024 d
1.025 a
1.026 Any order:
a. vowel sounds
b. consonant sounds
c. stress or accent
1.027 phonetics
1.028 schwa
1.029 false
1.030 true
1.031 false
1.032 true
1.033 false
1.034 k
1.035 c
1.036 l
1.037 b
1.038 h
1.039 i
1.040 a
1.041 g
1.042 e
1.043 d

SELF TEST 2

2.01 c
2.02 a
2.03 b
2.04 b
2.05 c
2.06 rence
2.07 ence
2.08 ance
2.09 ence
2.010 ance
2.011 ence
2.012 rence
2.013 ance
2.014 ence
2.015 ance
2.016 Either order:
a. des′ pic a ble
b. des pic′ a ble
2.017 Either order:
a. ex′ quis ite
b. ex quis′ ite
2.018 Either order:
a. ir ref′ u ta ble
b. ir ref u′ ta ble
2.019 b
2.020 d
2.021 c
2.022 a
2.023 c
2.024 c
2.025 c
2.026 d
2.027 a
2.028 b
2.029 mnemonic
2.030 rent
2.031 exaggerated pronunciation
2.032 memorized

SELF TEST 3

3.01 Example:
In Moscow Friday Jewish activist Anatoly Scharansky was sentenced to thirteen years in prison for high treason because of his activities as a spy for the United States.
3.02 fėr′ nus
3.03 kal′ vu ri
3.04 du brē′
3.05 ni mon′ iks
3.06 kaz′ um
3.07 e
3.08 i
3.09 a
3.010 j
3.011 k
3.012 l
3.013 b
3.014 d
3.015 f
3.016 g
3.017 a. meaning of the miracles
b. Christ died for us (optional)
c. the Resurrection
3.018 Example:
Helen denied the accusation and she angrily walked away.
3.019 Example:
Don't tease the dog or he will bite you.
3.020 Example:
I voted for the unpopular candidate, but my best friend didn't.
3.021 I wish I didn't have to go. I am very busy.

3.022 The cat chased a moth.
It knocked down a plant.
3.023 Pilate symbolically washed his hands. He knew that Christ was innocent.
3.024 An unstressed vowel.
3.025 short
3.026 long
3.027 measure
3.028 pencil
3.029 read (or reed)
3.030 star
3.031 music
3.032 prune
3.033 door
3.034 learn
3.035 mighty
3.036 glare

SELF TEST 1

1.01-1.06 Any order:
1.01 time order
1.02 spatial order
1.03 order of importance
1.04 comparison - contrast
1.05 cause - effect
1.06 simple listing
1.07 time order
1.08 cause - effect
1.09 spatial order
1.010 simple listing
1.011 order of importance
1.012 comparison - contrast
1.013 cause - effect
1.014 a. main idea (topic sentence)
b. supporting details
1.015 topic sentence
1.016 inferred
1.017 to explain or prove the main idea
1.018 first, at the beginning
1.019 ∇ inverted triangle
1.020 Δ regular triangle
1.021 ◇ diamond
1.022 □ rectangle
1.023 true
1.024 false
1.025 true
1.026 false
1.027 true
1.028 Topic sentence:
a. <u>The art of written discourse seems to have declined sharply in recent years</u>.
b. Shape ∇ inverted triangle
c. Pattern order of importance

SELF TEST 2

2.01-2.06 Any order:
2.01 Characterization - creating imaginary fictional people who seem real.
2.02 Plot - what happens; the sequence of events in a literary work.
2.03 Theme - the central idea of a work of literature
2.04 Language - the way the author uses his works; the diction, sentence structure and overall prose style of the story.
2.05 Setting - the location in place and time of the story.
2.06 Symbolism - the use of something that stands for or represents something else.
2.07 b
2.08 a
2.09 b
2.010 b
2.011 g
2.012 c
2.013 l
2.014 h
2.015 d
2.016 e
2.017 i
2.018 j
2.019 k
2.020 Describes a character who is a unique and particular individual but at the same time is representative of all men.

2.021 Of or having to do with space or area, occupying space.

2.022 A general statement inferred from particular facts.

2.023 Example:
A flat character has only one or two developed traits. Round, or well developed, characters are of two types: static and dynamic. A static character is not influenced by events around him. A dynamic character changes, or grows, according to the occurance in his life.

SELF TEST 3

3.01 Shan is dynamic.
3.02 Jo-Anne is flat.
3.03 Grace is static.
3.04 4
3.05 6
3.06 5
3.07 1
3.08 3
3.09 2
3.010 e
3.011 a
3.012 b
3.013 f
3.014 d
3.015 b
3.016 a
3.017 d
3.018 a
3.019 d
3.020 a
3.021 A character who does not change in response to events around him.
3.022 A character who changes as a result of what happens to him.
3.023 One who tells a story.
3.024 Figurative language that evokes mental pictures.
3.025 The main character in a play, story, or novel.

SELF TEST 1

1.01 singular
1.02 double negative
1.03 regular
1.04 family; herd; group; audience; team
1.05 e
1.06 c
1.07 d
1.08 f
1.09 a
1.010 drunk
1.011 lain
1.012 swum
1.013 a. worn
b. risen
1.014 past tense
1.015 present participle
1.016 third person singular
1.017 present participle
1.018 past tense
1.019 infinitive
1.020 past tense
1.021 infinitive
1.022 third person singular
1.023 present participle
1.024 We didn't eat any ice cream after all.
1.025 Nobody lost any time in getting to the game.
1.026 I never went there, either.
1.027 a noun that refers to more than one person or object; represents a collection of people, animals, or objects
1.028 a verb which does not form its past tense or its past participle by adding -ed

SELF TEST 2

2.01 a. singular
b. singular
2.02 a. terminational - adding -er or -est
b. analytical - using more or most
2.03 gerund
2.04 present participle
2.05 a. positive
b. comparative
c. superlative
2.06 Examples:
a. group
b. herd
2.07 regular
2.08 abler
2.09 most content
2.010 fittest
2.011 narrower
2.012 handsomest
2.013 seen; saw
2.014 laid; lain
2.015 begun; began
2.016 rode; ridden
2.017 a. spoke; spoken
b. set; sat
2.018 c
2.019 d
2.020 b
2.021 e
2.022 g
2.023 a
2.024 b
2.025 c
2.026 b
2.027 Seeing is believing.
2.028 Wishing is commanding.
2.029 Listening is understanding.

SELF TEST 3

3.01 rhythm

3.02 rhyme

3.03 antagonist

3.04 figure of speech

3.05 melodrama

3.06 hearing

3.07 rhythm

3.08 Any order:
   a. positive
   b. comparative
   c. superlative

3.09 Either order:
   a. adding -er or -est
   b. using more or most

3.010 Examples:
   a. team
   b. class

3.011 d or e

3.012 b

3.013 f

3.014 c

3.015 a

3.016 the part following the climax which resolves or explains the plot

3.017 a speech made by an actor to himself.

3.018 types, forms, or classifications of literature having specific characteristics

3.19 one of the dramatic forms which usually has a happy ending; does not have to be really funny

3.020 one of the dramatic forms which usually ends unhappily; often deals with death, failure, and similar topics

SELF TEST 1

1.01 b
1.02 b
1.03 a
1.04 a
1.05 a
1.06 b
1.07 a
1.08 b
1.09 a
1.010 a
1.011 chronologically
1.012 Either order:
  a. to persuade
  b. to inform
  or teach, convince, tell a story, analyze, criticize
1.013 topic
1.014 a. ascending
  b. descending
1.015 spatial
1.016 bandwagon
1.017 surrogate
1.018 sequence
1.019 analyze
1.020 implied
1.021 true
1.022 true
1.023 false
1.024 true
1.025 false
1.026 false
1.027 true
1.028 false
1.029 true
1.030 true
1.031-1.035 Examples:
1.031 The family's living conditions are deplorable.
1.032 Reading without comprehension is a waste of time.
1.033 More than one technique is employed in writing poetry.
1.034 The events in the poem were in chronological order.
1.035 Although we came in second, we will endeavor to be first next time.
1.036-1.040 Example:
1.036 a false idea or a misleading statement
1.037 machines, materials, and techniques used to meet human needs.
1.038 the condition or fact of being older; superiority in age or standing
1.039 use of one object to express or to stand for another
1.040 a substitute or stand-in

SELF TEST 2

2.01 true
2.02 false
2.03 true
2.04 false
2.05 true
2.06 true
2.07 false
2.08 true
2.09 true
2.010 false
2.011 true
2.012 false
2.013 visual aids
2.014 pictographs
2.015 pie graph
2.016 fallacy
2.017 logic

2.018 propaganda
2.019 emotionally charged
2.020 endorsements
2.021 f
2.022 d
2.023 m
2.024 k
2.025 a
2.026 i
2.027 l
2.028 c
2.029 b
2.030 e
2.031 h
2.032-2.041 Examples:
2.032 Too much sun is detrimental to one's skin.
2.033 The king's retinue was impressive.
2.034 Ellen is a proponent of health foods.
2.035 That movie has been censored in Boston.
2.036 We will incorporate that passage into the text.
2.037 The new business enterprise is developing well.
2.038 Public schools provide a secular education.
2.039 The two friends will honor the covenant.
2.040 The fog swirled ominously around the castle.
2.041 Seminaries include theology in their curriculums.
2.042 a
2.043 b
2.044 b
2.045 b
2.046 a
2.047 b
2.048 b
2.049 b
2.050 b
2.051-2.055 Examples:
2.051 (erroneous) Your facts are completely erroneous.
2.052 Mr. Wiley has seniority over us all.
2.053 (technique) The incorrect technique was applied.
2.054 The plant will not assimilate that fertilizer.
2.055 (enterprise) Free enterprise is supported here.
2.056

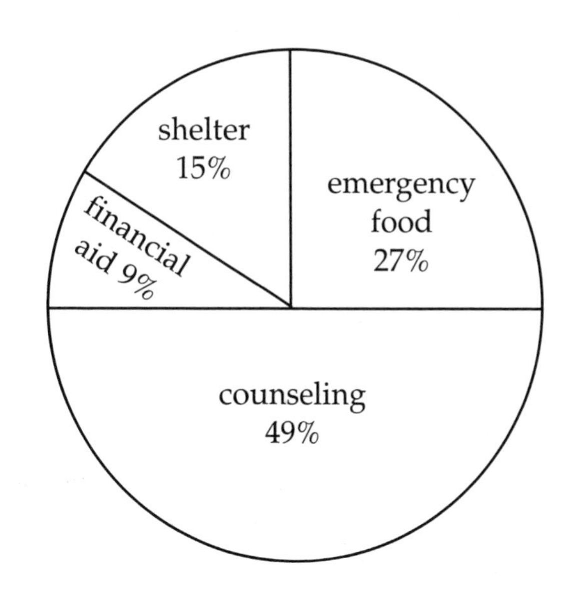

SELF TEST 3

3.01 f
3.02 h
3.03 k
3.04 m
3.05 j
3.06 a
3.07 b
3.08 e
3.09 c
3.010 l
3.011 g
3.012 d
3.013 n
3.014 true
3.015 false
3.016 true
3.017 true
3.018 false
3.019 true
2.020 true
3.021 false
3.022 false
3.023 true
3.024 synchronize
3.025 stanza
3.026 Shakespeare
3.027 meter
3.028 images
3.029 topic
3.030 reluctant
3.031 bar
3.032 visual aids
3.033 table
3.034-3.043 Example:
3.034 His concept of the problem was extraordinary.
3.035 Only in basketball is he my adversary.
3.036 All the subjects have been categorized.
3.037 Our natural resources are nearly depleted.
3.038 She implied that I was not honest.
3.039 Inhaling exhaust fumes is detrimental to health.
3.040 We have explicit orders.
3.041 The car is now operative.
3.042 That language is completely alien to me.
3.043 The industry's proponents of nuclear energy are numerous.
3.044 b
3.045 c
3.046 b
3.047 a
3.048 c

SELF TEST 1

1.01 true
1.02 true
1.03 false
1.04 false
1.05 true
1.06 false
1.07 true
1.08 false
1.09 false
1.010 true
1.011 be with thee!
1.012 . . . I will be thy mouth, and teach thee what thou shalt say.
1.013 Example:
very poor; He said he was slow of speech
1.014 who you are, or what you know
1.015 Any order:
- a. voice purity
- b. voice flexibility
- c. voice strength

1.016 Either order:
- a. subject
- b. attitude

1.017 Any order:
- a. to inform
- b. to impress
- c. to convince or persuade
- d. to entertain

1.018 Either order:
- a. conviction
- b. intelligence

1.019 Any order:
- a. sincerity
- b. friendliness
- c. authority

1.020 Either order:
- a. fear
- b. carelessness

1.021 amplifies tone
1.022 accuracy of tone
1.023 a solemn promise or pledge of loyalty
1.024 worn-out, overused
1.025 the state of being able to adapt to change
1.026 Examples; any order:
- a. remember the audience wants something
- b. remember the purposes: to inform, impress, persuade, entertain
- c. keep your audience guessing
- d. explain less; narrate more
- e. talk to the audience

or others given

1.027 Any order:
- a. Decide on the central idea and state it in one sentence.
- b. Choose the main points of your argument and arrange them in logical order.
- c. Select specific details.
- d. Map out the introduction.
- e. Outline the entire speech.
- or Plan the concluding statement and be sure that you move smoothly from one idea to another.

1.028
- a. age range
- b. the percentage of men, women, and children
- c. the kinds of professions represented
- d. the extent to which audience will be on your side
- e. education level

1.029
- a. size of the room
- b. likely distractions in the area
- c. how adequate the lighting will be
- d. whether there will be a platform
- e. the acoustics

or where you will speak, ventilation and temperature, will any equipment - - blackboard, projector - - be available if needed?

SELF TEST 2

2.01 false
2.02 false
2.03 true
2.04 false
2.05 true
2.06 false
2.07 true
2.08 true
2.09 true
2.010 false
2.011 read
2.012 a. near the front
b. eye
c. nod
2.013 listening
2.014 he is bored or uninterested
2.015 Any order:
a. that he is interested
b. that he is friendly
c. that he is cheerful
or he is relaxed, courteous, flexible, tactful
2.016 Examples:
a. weariness
b. anxiety
c. daydreaming
2.017 Examples:
a. loud music
b. an uncomfortable chair
c. a fidgety neighbor
2.018 Example:
Become excited about your subject; this excitement will utilize the energy productively. Keep your mind occupied with what you are going to say and how you could say it.
2.019 It is giving information as in many conversations. The speaker responds to audience reaction; he enjoys talking to them.
2.020 Example:
sincerity, by eye contact, voice tone, intentness; friendliness, by a twinkle in eye/voice and by looking at the people in the audience; authority, by obviously having facts that back up your thesis
2.021 Any five; any order:
Remember to keep your audience guessing; explain less; narrate more. Dramatize by giving them a challenge; put it up to them to do something. Organize your speech; find the real issue, but be conversational. Speak up in a lively manner so you can be heard. Put yourself in their place — they came for something; give it to them — but be yourself.
2.022 Example:
Most people hear what they want to hear, closing their ears to other information. If they feel the speaker has an ulterior motive, they will distort the message. If a speaker talks in unfamiliar language, listeners feel "put down."

2.023 Example:
All listening is affected by prior knowledge and also by the kind of material the speaker is using. The physiological activity of listening is a distinct part of listening. The concentration of the listener and the thoughts stirred up by the talk are vital.

2.024 b
2.025 a
2.026 d
2.027 b
2.028 d

SELF TEST 3

3.01 d
3.02 h
3.03 e
3.04 b
3.05 a
3.06 i
3.07 j
3.08 f
3.09 c
3.010 g
3.011 false
3.012 true
3.013 true
3.014 true
3.015 false
3.016 true
3.017 false
3.018 true
3.019 false
3.020 true
3.021 how sorry you are that you inconvenienced her and how much you enjoy her dinners (or appreciation for past kindnesses)
3.022 voice purity
3.023 Any order:
a. sincerity
b. friendliness
c. authority
3.024 Any order:
a. purity
b. flexibility
c. strength
3.025 Any order
a. that he is interested
b. that he is friendly
c. that he is cheerful
or relaxed, courteous, tactful
3.026 Any order:
a. loud music or noise
b. writing on blackboard
c. uncomfortable chair
or too cold/hot room
3.027 Any order:
a. use contractions
b. call the recipient by name
c. tell the recipient any news of his friends
d. answer the recipient's questions
e. let him know you are thinking of him
3.028 Any order:
a. for a birthday gift
b. for a Christmas gift
c. for a weekend visit
d. apology for not accepting an

invitation
e. note of congratulations or note of condolence

3.029 reading back over a paper or a letter to check for content and grammar

3.030 Example:
A business letter should be able to state concisely the purpose of the letter; it should build good will for the sender. It should be accurate in every part; it should provide all of the information required. It should be brief, condensed. It should be clear. It can serve as a record of transaction.

SELF TEST 1

1.01 f
1.02 g
1.03 i
1.04 j
1.05 a
1.06 h
1.07 c
1.08 b
1.09 e
1.010 d
1.011 encyclopedia
1.012 gazetteer
1.013 English or British
1.014 Any order:
- a. author
- b. title
- c. subject

1.015 a. size
- b. the more information it contains, the more likely it will serve the needs of its users

1.016 a. its frequency of revision or supplements
- b. the English language is constantly changing and a current dictionary should reflect contemporary usage

1.017 Any order:
- a. the encyclopedia
- b. the card catalog
- c. the *Reader's Guide*

1.018 librarians
1.019 b
1.020 b
1.021 b
1.022 b
1.023 c

SELF TEST 2

2.01 c
2.02 f
2.03 a
2.04 e
2.05 b
2.06 flat
2.07 stage directions
2.08 thesaurus
2.09 round
2.010 Any order:
- a. himself
- b. man
- c. society
- d. environment

2.011 card catalog
2.012 exposition
2.013 periodicals
2.014 themes
2.015 etymology
2.016 denouement
2.017 setting
2.018 b
2.019 b
2.020 b
2.021 c
2.022 a

SELF TEST 3

3.01 e
3.02 g
3.03 c
3.04 f
3.05 d
3.06 h
3.07 a
3.08 1880's
3.09 synonym
3.010 obedience
3.011 blindness
3.012 twenty
3.013 water
3.014 touching hand to cheek
3.015 Any order:
- a. subject
- b. author
- c. title

3.016 c
3.017 a
3.018 c
3.019 a
3.020 c
3.021 c
3.022 c
3.023 c
3.024 *Reader's Guide to Periodical Literature*
3.025 Either order:
- a. Library of Congress system
- b. Dewey Decimal system

3.026 *Oxford English Dictionary*
3.027 Any order:
- a. plot
- b. characters
- c. setting
  or theme, style, structure, stage directions.

SELF TEST 1

1.01 true
1.02 true
1.03 false
1.04 true
1.05 true
1.06 false
1.07 false
1.08 true
1.09 true
1.010 true
1.011 e
1.012 k
1.013 a
1.014 h
1.015 g
1.016 c
1.017 j
1.018 b
1.019 f
1.020 i
1.021 b
1.022 a
1.023 c
1.024 b
1.025 a
1.026 c
1.027 a
1.028 c
1.029 b
1.030 a
1.031 Either order:
a. mystery
b. fantasy
1.032 letters
1.033 Robinson Crusoe
1.034 Any order:
a. romanticism
b. impressionism
c. expressionism
d. realism
1.035 a. animal
b. fights for survival
1.036 Either order:
a. clear
b. direct
1.037 traditional rules and customs of a group of people
1.038 a story or account
1.039 expressing or naming a quality, idea, or concept

SELF TEST 2

2.01 true
2.02 true
2.03 false
2.04 false
2.05 true
2.06 true
2.07 true
2.08 false
2.09 false
2.010 true
2.011 k
2.012 f
2.013 a
2.014 h
2.015 b
2.016 j
2.017 g
2.018 c

2.019 i
2.020 d
2.021 b
2.022 a
2.023 a
2.024 b
2.025 a
2.026 c
2.027 b
2.028 a
2.029 b
2.030 a
2.031 Arthur or Arthurian legend
2.032 Either order:
  a. Charlemagne
  b. William of Orange
2.033 Any order:
  a. Alexander the Great
  b. city of Thebes
  c. city of Troy
2.034 Either order:
  a. English
  b. Germanic or German
2.035 first person
2.036 a. climax
  b. resolution
2.037 suspense
2.038 a character that undergoes little or no change in the progress of the story
2.039 a character that undergoes changes within the action and whose changes are shown with the consequences
2.040 Example:
Plot usually centers on character. Those incidents that arise naturally from the characters present an effective plot that shows a struggle in which the characters engage.

SELF TEST 3

3.01 false
3.02 true
3.03 true
3.04 true
3.05 false
3.06 true
3.07 true
3.08 false
3.09 false
3.010 true
3.011 f
3.012 a
3.013 k
3.014 g
3.015 b
3.016 j
3.017 d
3.018 h
3.019 c
3.020 e
3.021 Any order:
  a. to know the text
  b. to select a topic
  c. to outline material
  d. to find evidence
  e. to write the essay
3.022 gothic
3.023 novel of manners

3.024 historical

3.025 regional

3.026 Any order:

a. a work of fantasy

b. breaks away from reality

c. based on science fact or assumption or takes place in an unreal world

3.027 Example:
form of writing that uses letters as the means of relating the action

3.028 Example:
novel that deals with a single social class, its manners, customs, mores, habits, and so forth; presents its class accurately and in detail

3.029 Example:
novel that reconstructs the past based on scholarship

3.030 Example:
novel that works out a central problem through characters or incidents

3.031 Example:
to analyze, to take things apart in order to determine their worth, to evaluate the material, to find the meaning of all the parts and the whole

3.032 Example:
means of organizing material and thoughts, and helps writer to see organization and any flaws that may occur

SELF TEST 1

1.01 true
1.02 true
1.03 true
1.04 false
1.05 true
1.06 false
1.07 false
1.08 false
1.09 true
1.010 false
1.011 lives
1.012 potatoes
1.013 messes
1.014 bunches
1.015 radios
1.016 John's
1.017 the players'
1.018 horse's
1.019 policemen's
1.020 girl friend's
1.021 transitive
1.022 intransitive
1.023 transitive
1.024 intransitive
1.025 intransitive
1.026 appositive phrase
1.027 gerund phrase
1.028 infinitive phrase
1.029 correlative conjunction
1.030 participial phrase
1.031 morphology
1.032 Any order:
a. written
b. spoken
c. nonverbal
1.033 Any order:
a. positive
b. comparative
c. superlative
1.034 Any order:
a. attributive
b. appositive
c. predicate
1.035 a. six
b. conjugation
1.036 voice
1.037 Any order:
a. indicative
b. subjunctive
c. imperative
1.038 a common noun referring to a quality or idea that cannot be seen or touched
1.039 a noun standing for more than one person, place, or thing, such as team
1.040 when the pronunciation of vowels changed in Middle English, resulting in the diphthongal glide and certain unusual spellings or pronunciations
1.041 the way words are put together to form sentences
1.042 a
1.043 c
1.044 b
1.045 a

SELF TEST 2

2.01 p.a.
2.02 i.o.
2.03 d.o.
2.04 s
2.05 p
2.06 p.n.
2.07 p.a.
2.08 i.o.
2.09 s
2.010 d.o.
2.011 simple
2.012 compound
2.013 simple
2.014 complex
2.015 compound
2.016 Any order:
 a. heading
 b. inside address
 c. salutation
 d. body
 e. closing
 f. signature
2.017 f
2.018 i
2.019 b
2.020 c
2.021 g
2.022 e
2.023 d
2.024 a
2.025 k
2.026 h
2.027 The girl in the brown sweater is my best friend.

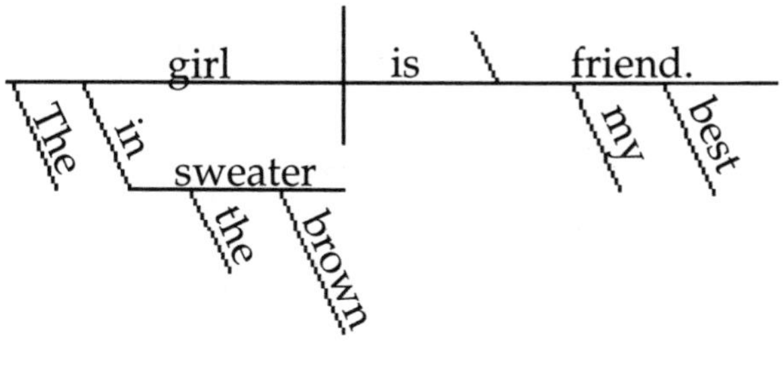

girl | is \ friend.
The
in
sweater
the
brown
my
best

2.028 true
2.029 false
2.030 false
2.031 true
2.032 true
2.033 false
2.034 true
2.035 false
2.036 false
2.037 false
2.038 Indo-European
2.039 Chaucer
2.040 English
2.041 subjunctive
2.042 an apostrophe and s
2.043 an adjective
2.044 a. radios
 b. calves
 c. cities
2.045 a. her sister-in-law's
 b. boys'
 c. her
2.046 a. have
 b. had
 c. had
2.047 a. transitive
 b. transitive
 c. intransitive
2.048 a. adjective clause
 b. adverb clause
 c. adverb clause
 d. noun clause

SELF TEST 3

3.01 false
3.02 true
3.03 false
3.04 false
3.05 false
3.06 false
3.07 true
3.08 true
3.09 true
3.010 false
3.011 f
3.012 a
3.013 j
3.014 i
3.015 l
3.016 k
3.017 h
3.018 c
3.019 g
3.020 b
3.021 e
3.022 d
3.023 Any order:
  a. recognize the words
  b. attach meaning to the words
  c. fuse the meanings into an idea
  d. dig out the implied meanings
  e. react to what was read
3.024 logic vs. emotion
3.025 either—or
3.026 jumping on the bandwagon
3.027 endorsement
3.028 an organizational method whereby events are described in the order that they occurred; time sequence
3.029 a verbal ending in *-ing* and functioning as a noun
3.030 has a subject and predicate but does not express a complete thought
3.031 is made up of a main clause and one or more subordinate (dependent) clauses
3.032 arranged in normal order: subject, predicate, object; the main thought is presented first
3.033 card catalog
3.034 an abstract
3.035 passive voice
3.036 antecedent
3.037 Any order;
  a. coordinating conjunctions
  b. subordinating conjunctions
  c. correlative conjunctions
  d. conjunctive adverbs
3.038 imperative
3.039 Listening to hymns is my favorite pastime.

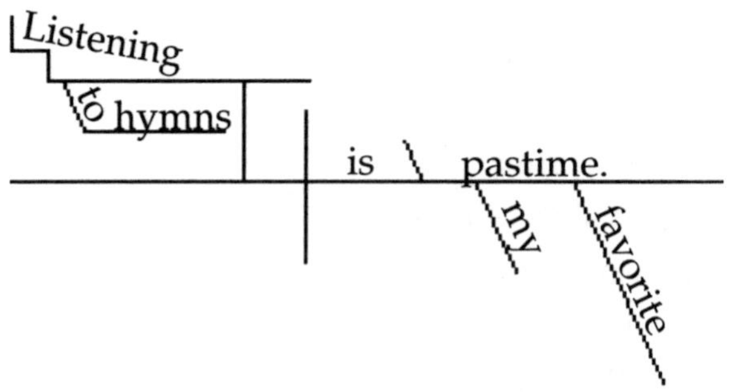

Listening
to hymns
is \ pastime.
my
favorite

3.040 Example:
Sound is trapped by the outer ear. Sound is transmitted by vibration of the ear drum (tympanic membrane) in the middle ear, and the bones (malleus, incus and stapes) transmit the vibrations through the semicircular canal to the inner ear and cochlea containing nerves, and on to the brain.
3.041 i.o.
3.042 p.n.
3.043 p.a.
3.044 s.
3.045 s.
3.046 c
3.047 a
3.048 b

1. true
2. false
3. false
4. true
5. true
6. false
7. true
8. false
9. false
10. true
11. c
12. e
13. i
14. k
15. a
16. m
17. b
18. o
19. d
20. l
21. j
22. h
23. n
24. g
25. nominative
26. conjunction
27. two
28. pairs
29. sentence
30. i.o.
31. p.a.
32. s.
33. d.o.
34. p.
35. d
36. c
37. b
38. a
39.

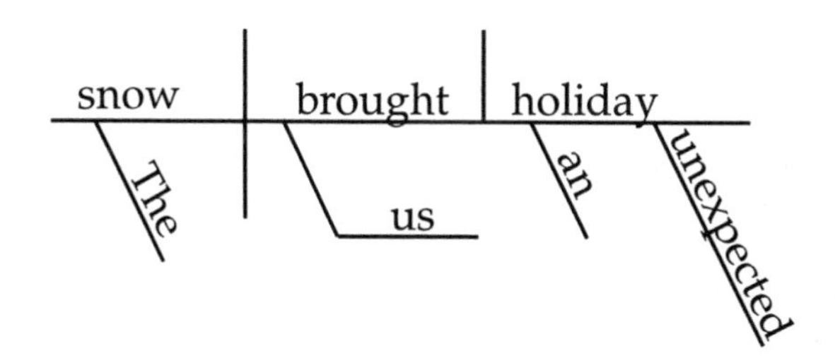

1. c
2. f
3. g
4. e
5. a
6. d
7. true
8. true
9. false
10. true
11. false
12. a
13. b
14. a
15. b
16. c
17. d
18. a
19. b
20. c
21. b
22. b
23. Abraham
24. human
25. second
26. a. Indus
    b. Europe
27. a. Latin
    b. Indo-European
28. Germanic (or Anglo-Saxon)
29. second
30. parts of speech
31. Hint:
    You should have mentioned all of the things common to all true language. Animals cannot acquire any of these because of their physical and mental limitations.

1. dī′ u krĭt′ u kul, diacritical
2. ni mon′ iks, mnemonics
3. fō net′ iks, phonetics
4. des pik′ a bul or des′ pik a bul, despicable
5. ir ref′ u ta ble or ir ref u′ ta ble
6. kom′ u, comma
7. tu mid′ u ti, timidity
8. state
9. bait
10. feel
11. learn
12. dodge
13. tune
14. pair or pear, pare
15. stair (or stare)
16. pull
17. fudge
18. c
19. a
20. c
21. d
22. c
23. a
24. c
25. b
26. d
27. b
28. usually
29. c
30. athletic
31. c
32. lightning
33. c
34. mathematics
35. c
36. February
37. c
38. f
39. a
40. e
41. b
42. d
43. c
44. Hint:
    All five points should be included in one sentence.
    Example:
    Colonel J. O. Hanford, Williams Air Force Base commander, said Wednesday that he fears that the lifting of a state ban against construction in a nearby area, will result in homes being built in a "crash potential zone."
45. Example:
    They lead the reader smoothly from one point to the next.

1. generalization
2. contrast
3. comparison or comparison-contrast
4. topic sentence
5. supporting details
6. e
7. d
8. b
9. f
10. c
11. a
12. b.
13. c.
14. b.
15. c.
16. b.
17. c.
18. plot
19. theme
20. setting
21. language

1. d
2. k
3. j
4. a
5. f
6. g
7. b
8. e
9. c
10. h
11. poetry
12. the short story
13. tragedy
14. characters
15. double negative
16. a noun
17. an adjective
18. a. better
    b. best
19. a. bad
    b. worse
20. a. taller
    b. tallest
21. a. did
    b. done
22. a. to go
    b. gone
23. a. lay
    b. lain
24. a. to throw
    b. threw
25. is
26. Is; its
27. had bitten
28. most sacred
29. drier
30. More blessed
31. Skiing can be great fun. Speeding down the slopes can also be dangerous. Skiing accidents are common. Purchasing or renting good skiing equipment is important.

1. e
2. j
3. h
4. g
5. a
6. k
7. b
8. i
9. d
10. c
11. true
12. true
13. false
14. true
15. true
16. false
17. true
18. true
19. true
20. false
21. pie graph
22. tetrameter
23. topic
24. images
25. graph
26. anapest
27. free verse
28. true rhyme
29. iambic feet
30. tetra-

31-40 Examples:

31. Your evidence is erroneous.
32. The plight of the striving people is deplorable.
33. They implied that we were accepted.
34. The chemicals have a detrimental reaction.
35. He will censor the magazines.
36. The puppy's surrogate mother was a cat.
37. All the machinery is operative.
38. I felt like an alien at the party.
39. Endeavor to make personal improvements.
40. The juvenile stood in line at the theatre.
41. To go uninvited is inappropriate.
42. (sentinel) The sentinel stopped us at the gate.
43. Statistics is a difficult course.
44. (analysis) My analysis is incomplete.
45. He tried to assimilate the directions.
46. I will incorporate your ideas.
47. (exaggeration) He is guilty of exaggeration.
48. We will assess the value of the property.
49. The list was in chronological order.
50. The plan has my endorsement.

1. false
2. true
3. true
4. true
5. true
6. true
7. false
8. false
9. true
10. false
11. d
12. b
13. a
14. d
15. b
16. d
17. a
18. f
19. g
20. m
21. b
22. c
23. h
24. i
25. e
26. k
27. d
28. a
29. l

30-33 Examples:

30. liking them, being honest, enthusiastic
31. being relaxed, not stiff
32. attaches new information to prior thoughts
33. saying something personal, expressing felt appreciation
34. Moses
35. Any order:
    a. purity
    b. flexibility
    c. strength
36. speaking
37. voice purity
38. listening

39-40 Examples:

39. The way we say things shows how we feel about them. Our body movements tell whether we mean what we say. A sense of humor is bound to show through.
40. worry about a test, things at home, a date, concern about an upcoming appointment, something future
41. Write the way you talk; write about the things you would talk about if the one you are writing were with you.
42. appreciation, accuracy, brevity, clarity, promptness

1. d
2. c
3. f
4. a
5. b
6. Renaissance
7. climax
8. stage directions
9. obedience
10. associated the word <u>water</u> with water
11. using the *New York Times Index*
12. encyclopedia
13. card catalog
14. bibliography
15. Greece
16. dictionary
17. false
18. true
19. true
20. false
21. true
22. b
23. c
24. c
25. a
26. b

1. false
2. true
3. true
4. true
5. false
6. true
7. true
8. true
9. false
10. true
11. e
12. k
13. a
14. b
15. f
16. j
17. h
18. d
19. g
20. c
21. b
22. a
23. a
24. b
25. c
26. c
27. a
28. b
29. c
30. a
31. opposition
32. crisis
33. mistrusts
34. Either order:
    a. power
    b. revenge
35. pastoral elegy
36. author
37. prose
38. teller
39. Troilus and Criseyde
40. a. many headed monster
    b. sea dragon
       or serpent, too big to fish for
41. Example:
    character that changes little or
    not at all
42. Example:
    character that undergoes changes
    within the actions of the novel;
    characters whose changes are shown
    with the consequences
43. Example:
    not restricted by time, place, or
    character; moves and comments at will
44. Example:
    The vantage point from which the
    reader is given the materials in
    the story.

1. true
2. true
3. false
4. false
5. false
6. true
7. true
8. false
9. true
10. true
11. l
12. h
13. c
14. b
15. d
16. e
17. j
18. k
19. g
20. i
21. a
22. f
23. Any order:
    a. a pattern of sounds
    b. a collection of words
    c. a system of word arrangement
    d. elements of grammar
24. Any order:
    a. be natural
    b. be enthusiastic
    c. use illustration
    d. speak clearly
    e. have a purpose
25. Any order:
    a. informal
    b. social
    c. business
26. a. the card catalog
    b. *The Reader's Guide*
    c. an encyclopedia
27. a. girl
    b. was elected
    c. queen
    d. of rodeo
    e. the